# SENSING PLACE

For Richard and Oscar

Philip Gumuchdjian

# SENSING PLACE

## What is the point of architecture?

eightbooks

Published in 2019 by
Eight Books Limited
40 Herbert Gardens
London NW10 3BU
info@8books.co.uk
www.8books.co.uk

Design by Praline
www.designbypraline.com

Typeset in ER Canto
www.renno.info/canto

A catalogue record for this book is available
from the British Library.

ISBN 978-1-9998583-7-7
Printed in The Netherlands

Foreword by Niall McLaughlin 6

Introduction 8

Sensing Place 11
  Think Tank 14
  Film Den 22
  Dacha 24
  The Butler Collection 30
  Marsh House 34
  El Mirador 38
  Eyrie 44
  Heckfield Place 46

The Past Is a Present 49
  The Fort 52
  Echo House 54
  Edwin Lutyens at Piccadilly 56
  Wells Coates at 10 Palace Gate 58
  Richard Rogers at Wimbledon 60
  Villa, Glebe Place 66
  William Chambers at Wick House 72

It's All in the Detail 79

Home Is Where the Hearth Is 103

Everything but the Building 127
  London as it could be 130
  Albertopolis 2025 134
  Cities for a small planet 136
  Giant Recycled Paper Building 138
  St Marylebone School 144
  Youth Club 158
  Tate Tower 160
  Market Place 168
  Centre Pompidou-Metz 170
  Public Library 176
  Tread Lightly 180

Conclusion 186

Biography 188
Collaborators 190
Thanks 191

When I drive out west in County Cork, I always look for Philip's little riverside house. It is one of my markers, measuring the two-hour journey into familiar stages. As the road skirts above the River Ilen for a few miles, I look down to catch a glimpse. It is curious, because I know it is not visible from the road, but I see people in skiffs rowing on the stream and I know that they can see it. So, in a way, I sense it is there and I feel as if I have seen it. I intuit its steady presence on the water and I apprehend that it is a hidden part of the same scene that I am passing through. This is the power of good architecture to hold a landscape and to change it, allowing us to imaginatively occupy it in ways that would not otherwise be possible. Flying by in my car, I am at once looking down on this little hut, I am inside it and I am watching it from the water below. It is like a concealed pin that holds and structures the fall of a garment.

Not many buildings have that power and it is worth asking why this one does. It is an ordered frame below a roof and it creates a small moment where shelter and exposure are held in balance on the threshold between land and water. In a place of shift and flux it is intentionally held in stillness: frame and roof, openness and protection, compression and release. The architectural device used to achieve this is a simple supporting structure expressed with clarity. When I drive by, imagining the hidden building, this is what I see: wooden posts and beams holding up a roof on the edge of an empty expanse.

The supporting frame is the thing in Philip's buildings. It is what he employs to bring reason to the complex and competing array of influences that present themselves in every project. He uses it as a musician would use the base line. It provides the tempo and the subliminal sense of purpose. It doesn't just support the construction, or frame the inhabitation, it stands for the idea of reasonableness itself. Architecture is an act of public reasoning and it gains authority by demonstrating its arguments in a formally lucid fashion. For this architect, the calm, logical and regular supporting lattice is evidence of the validity of his thinking. It is intended to bring everything else into an ordered arrangement.

In placing a structure in a landscape, Philip attends to the broader environment: its history and lineaments; the views to and from the building and those pockets of warm shelter brought about by the natural lie of the land. This is an act of great delicacy and architectural tact. The building needs to seem as if it has always been there and yet its effect is one of transformation. The new landscape that emerges must seem as if it could never have been without the building.

The natural world and the world of human artefacts have grown together over millennia. It no longer makes sense to speak of unspoilt nature. Hope for the future lies in new ideas of stewardship in which land and buildings are cultivated together as part of a continuity. It is possible to imagine new kinds of balance between our activities and the land which forms the ground for our imaginings. The projects in this book offer themselves as examples of a form of thinking that sees the buildings we make as part of a longer duration in which our constructions are constantly open to alteration, change and re-invention. The goal of the architect is not as a maker of conceptually finite forms, but as a participant in open-ended processes that last over generations.

The case studies in this book are a demonstration of the skill of the architect. Philip is

constantly looking for the hidden order
in things and situations. He seeks out common
themes in human activities and uses them
to create frames for these activities. The act
of framing is at once responsive and generative.
It situates the human imagination and opens
up new possibilities, new ways of being in
a place. This can occur at the level of individual
buildings, urban plans or broader strategic
thinking. The trajectory of this book is from the
particular and situated, to the broader realm
of general strategy. It shows someone who
has an appetite to build lucid representations
of public reasoning as a foundation for our
individual experiences and our civil society.

The invitation to exhibit twenty years of architectural output means I can begin to join the dots and literally spell out the ideas that underpin our work. Those ideas form the DNA of our projects but more often remain hidden in plain sight. The need for explanation exposes the main paradox of an art form that has ambitions to communicate but by being inherently mute is entirely reliant on the poetics of form and space to do so.

Buildings are condemned to speak our thoughts in hushed tones of scale, form and texture. Thoughts we seek to express flow through the senses and, initially at least, bypass the intellect. We manipulate space and form to provoke emotions and stimulate sensibilities all in the hope of sharing our own perceptions with others.

And despite the most diligent efforts during the multiple years of the buildings' incubation, its physical intrusion into common reality bestows on all onlookers the right of instantaneous judgement without so much as a caption to lead the way. This is the lot of any work of architecture and whilst we acknowledge that buildings should not have to rely on explanations, we also must admit they do gain from a modicum of deciphering.

This book catalogues the maelstrom of concurrent and competing ideas that underpin a typical body of architectural work but that are barely readable by the passer-by. My work is driven by observation, analysis as well as emotional response, and it is all of these perspectives that fuel my design intuition and fundamental belief in the necessity to respect our shared human past.

Observation and common sense under-score my approach to our pressing need to be as environmentally gentle as possible.

I aim to develop resource-efficient, environ-mental systems that make best use of whatever free energies are available, be they contained in the light, the air, the earth or its plants. I openly borrow from the past and use talented engineers to work out systems that save resources wherever they can.

The architectural solutions we develop are therefore a mix of observation and invention. Like a writer or a painter we observe the world and bring those observations to bear albeit after exhaustive and cold-hearted analysis of practicability and affordability. I hope that airing the broad span of sensitivities and ambitions that form the foundations of an architectural project will reveal unnoticed nuances and stimulate the reader's mind.

Lastly I hope that my advocacy of the relevance and importance of architecture to everyday mainstream life will persuade the reader and also gain nodding approval from my fellow architects who at this very moment in countries far and wide are sweating at the coal face, exploring new ways that we dream will encourage the betterment of the lives of people on this environmentally depleted, socially inequitable and commercially over-exploited planet.

# SENSING PLACE

The best buildings reveal
the spirit of a place.

It all started with an unremarkable gesture. Night was falling, the weather was closing in, I was alone on the edge of the Isle of Grain. The wind and rain in my face, the sea at my back, no civilisation in sight save for a massive petrochemical plant. A more alien environment this young Londoner could not have imagined.

The tarpaulin was flapping uncontrollably in the wind, the night-long vigil was in peril and with it my response to the first of many incomprehensible student assignments set by the inimitable John Andrews for which I had spent a full month designing, fabricating and planning.

And then as if by magic the tent deployed, the stays held and a pure conical form emerged to wrestle a dry and temperate interior from the hostile windswept outdoors. A powerful moment that viscerally connected me to the most primordial of human actions: the creation of shelter.

As evening settled into night, I set out my equipment: lamp, heater, paintbrushes, colour pigments and binding medium. The tipi's skin provided both defence from the elements and a canvas onto which I was to record my impressions and feelings.

The night passed in a dogged battle between my reluctance to attempt a first mark, my paints and the flapping, stain-repelling PVC tarpaulin. To make matters worse the propane heater and lamp were generating enough moisture to ensure a constant flow of condensation on the inner side of the tent, which guaranteed that my first forays into painting were dissolving in front of my eyes as fast as I could apply them. Several hours passed in what felt like a futile battle with the elements until I noticed that the storm had abated.

As I stepped out into the darkness, the sounds of the land came alive around me. I wandered into the landscape and over the dyke to the beach beyond where the glistening estuary reached out from its muddy flats to the open sea beyond. To be alone in this vast, open world was somehow both poignant and elating, both melancholic and life-confirming. The flatness of the territory and the sheer immensity of the night sky bore powerfully down and drilled into me a deep sense of belonging and connection to the planet.

And as I turned back, the tipi had unexpectedly turned into a glowing lantern. I had stepped out of an internalised space but as darkness prevailed this inner world had become a beacon on the landscape, calmly expressing and broadcasting the safety of its 'haven'.

But more surprises were to follow. Hours of work later, exhausted and thoroughly dispirited by my ham-fisted painterly exploits, I suddenly noticed that a golden aura was beginning to infuse the work and lend it a coherence and beauty. The dawn had crept up on the artist and as a reward for his efforts the sun had finished off what the artist could not do by bathing the translucent surfaces of the tent in the warm glow of returning life.

We all have experiences of being in nature. Most lie dormant in our individual memories. But parts of these experiences are shared over the centuries and, I believe, reside in our collective memory and are passed on through our common DNA.

Forty years on I can still feel the intensity of that moment of communion and I am still working today to instil my buildings with that capacity to connect people to their place.

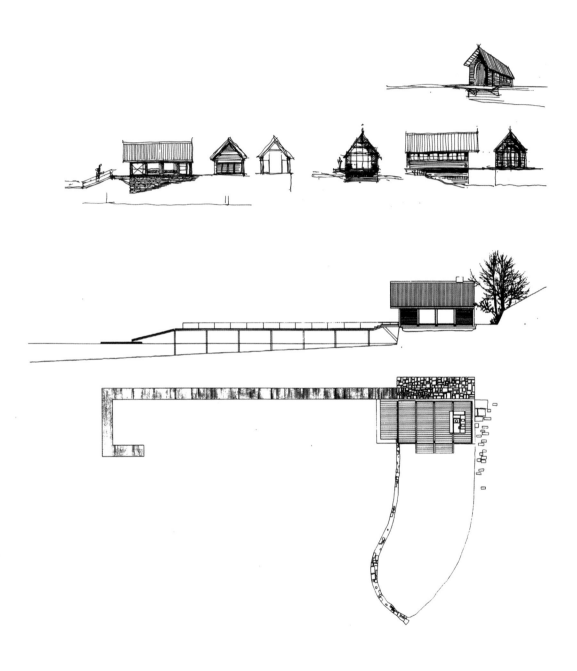

*Think Tank, Skibbereen, County Cork, Ireland:* My first building commission was a riverside dayhouse in County Cork. The client had purchased a farmhouse on a spectacular piece of land that cascaded down into the tidal River Ilen that connects the town of Skibbereen to the Atlantic Ocean.

The Irish sky alternated between outbursts of drenching rain and heavenly shafts of 'cathedral' sunlight. I was bowled over by the inestimable beauty of the place and equally certain that adding another building was the last thing that this magnificent landscape required. While conjuring up winning arguments to convince the client to leave all well alone, I was introduced to the man who would build my design, and my escape route was closed off. Bill Wolfe had grown up locally and had spent a lifetime building without an architect. There was little to indicate that he needed one now, especially one from London. We shook hands and were left alone to get started. Bill was a master of traditional construction and a man of few words. I was on the threshold of designing my first very precise and very modern building. It took the best part of two years of collaboration to win him over and cement a deep sense of trust and mutual respect.

Before the building was even designed, our urgent task was to make a constructive start as the planning permission was about to lapse. To those unacquainted with this art it is in equal parts worrying and exhilarating. A bit more to the left, a bit further into the river, a slight twist here to get a better view from that spot, etc, etc. and not the least of the problems was that the tide kept changing the geometry of the site; moving up and down, in and out. Eventually we settled on a position that was marked by Bill with large stakes hammered into the river bed from a boat. Bill then convened a meeting with his local friends to ascertain the ideal vertical position of the building. Low enough to sense the presence of the river but not so low as to allow a stormy spring tide to flood the structure. The men assembled and recounted jocular tales of floods gone by and eventually we settled on an altitude marked by a cast-iron bench that all agreed had never been submerged.

Having set out the structure the client sailed me up and down the river. Seen from the farmhouse the site was private and secluded. Seen from the water the site was exposed and public. It became obvious that a building on this site would become a public landmark and should integrate rather than stand out from the series of boathouses that peppered the river banks and acted as way-markers for

*Previous*
First mark — the tipi on the Isle of Grain.

*Opposite*
Sketches of traditional boathouses transform into final architectural drawings.

*Think Tank, Skibbereen*

its many users. As such the whole undertaking was as much a public domain project as it was a secluded private space for its owner.

I resolved to embrace a traditional form and to re-work it into a discernibly late 20th-century work, to marry the benefits of a contemporary glass house with the approachability of an evocative traditional structure. The decision was reinforced by the natural conditions of the site. Skibbereen enjoys an annual rainfall that is double that of London. It has to withstand storms that are fierce enough to preclude all construction over the winter months. The building is exposed and isolated. A pitched roof was therefore a natural choice despite, hard to believe today, its vernacular reference being considered at the time (1998) a Modernist heresy.

The early sketches follow a process of distilling the essential character from the traditional boathouses I had observed along the river until a metamorphosis from traditional to a modern hybrid design was achieved. To my mind, a building that sat in the river had to do justice to its privileged siting and immerse the senses of the occupant in the river. I likened the experience I was aiming to achieve to that of a fly-fisherman standing in waders and sensing the flow of the tide.

Glass replaced traditional stone walls, just as red cedar timber, that silvered beautifully, replaced their slate roofs. The overhanging roof became the dominant element from within, from above and from long views. The roof was treated as an independent element placed onto the structure: sliced off at the back and greatly cantilevered forward into the prevailing winds to afford the greatest protection from the river-borne gales. The roof gave a sense of comfort during storms and deep shade during the summer when the windows were open. Unlike a flat roof, the pitched shape created a hierarchy between the views. A giant gabled end faced across the stream, with smaller framed views looking upstream and sideways into an intimate freshwater pond.

The overriding design concern was to protect the simplicity and clarity of the main structure so as to project the sense of the building being nothing more than an open timber barn-like framework. Achieving this took meticulous care with every detail, especially the frames of the fixed, sliding and casement windows that were fabricated in stainless steel, minimised to the nth degree and wherever possible let into the timber columns to disappear from view.

The sequence of entering and moving towards the great glass gable was carefully choreographed to provide a dramatic sequence

*Opposite*
Think Tank immersed in its spectacular riverside setting.

*Overleaf left*
The entrance sequence is carefully controlled to heighten the experience.

*Overleaf right*
A side deck hovers over a small reflecting pool. The cedar roof is alternately bleached by the sun and darkened by the rain.

*Think Tank, Skibbereen*

*Think Tank, Skibbereen*

towards a framed view of epic proportions. To provide a degree of privacy within this exposed transparent structure, we installed panels of horizontal timber slats asymmetrically around the structure. These simple elements added a surprising variety of visual experiences, some more intimate, some more focused.

The project, its accessibility, success and recognition, focused my mind on two fundamental lines of exploration: the first being the distillation of ideas from traditional architecture, the second a deepening interest in the art of integrating buildings within their settings.

*Opposite*
Buildings can augment the experience of the landscape if all details are meticulously controlled.

*Film Den, Skibbereen*

_Film Den, Skibbereen, County Cork, Ireland:_ A follow-up commission to add a projection room to the farmhouse gave Bill and me an opportunity to evolve a response to the ubiquitous problem of extending buildings and doing so without simply adding more clutter to the original house.

The people of the southern Mediterranean volcanic island of Pantelleria use dry-stone walls to tame the wilderness, to shelter crops from the wind and to create habitable open courtyards and enclosures. These stone structures cover the entire island. One particular wall had caught my attention as it started as a low property marker, transformed itself to enclose a private garden wall, opened to form an archway entrance and then became the side of a farmhouse. This simple structure read as an uncomplicated single element but actually performed several very different functions.

I exploited this simple device to enclose the new room within a network of dry-stone walls that contained the clutter of extensions that had already accumulated around the old building. The new primary wall formed a new entrance courtyard and included an arch that led to the greenhouses, conservatory and rear gardens beyond and then fused into the garden. The new screening room was set within this arrangement of walls without reading as an independent building that would have diluted the dominance of the main farmhouse. This was an example of expanding the scope of a brief to enhance the overall setting.

As for the study/screening room, the challenge was to avoid designing a black box and instead open the room to the garden without undermining its function as a cinema. The project was therefore the total inverse of the extrovert Think Tank. Our aim was to focus on the enclosed space and only admit chinks of light and views. Having laid out the enclosing garden walls to restructure the outer spaces of the house, we conceived the enclosing roof of the screening room as a floating timber structure that spanned from the main house all the way to the projection screen where it landed on two small pin joints. The gap between the roof and the walls was left empty, but the space was enclosed by a continuous unframed infill of glass. The daylight from those slits brightens the room and can be easily shuttered off for projections. It creates a dramatic halo of light around the perimeter of the room and a luminous proscenium arch with framed garden vignettes (see pages 96–97).

_Opposite_
The new dry-stone wall encloses the entrance courtyard and conceals the screening room.

*Dacha, Lake Seliger*

*Dacha, Lake Seliger, Russia:* In 2011 we received an invitation to prepare designs for a dacha on Lake Seliger on the edge of the Valdaysky National Park midway between Moscow and St Petersburg. The site edged the same waters in which President Putin once famously celebrated Epiphany with an icy dip.

As we drove from Moscow through the endless flat landscape, my thoughts inevitably turned to the plight of the infamous invading and retreating armies lost in a similar wilderness of silver birch forests, harassed by Cossacks and with no views ahead save for more forest. After several hours of driving, the seemingly interminable forest gave way to clearings and then eventually to the water's edge. As our gaze adjusted to embrace the expanse of lake and its glimmering golden domed churches, the feeling of intense release was palpable.

The brief for the dacha was spartan. A weekend retreat in which the owner and his young family wanted to be entirely immersed in the landscape.

We worked to fuse the architectural concept with the landscape so that neither would take precedence over the other. Michel Desvigne, the landscape architect with whom I had collaborated on the design of the legacy parks that run the length of the Greenwich Peninsula, developed an intriguing approach. A great admirer of Frederick Law Olmsted, whose many creations include New York's Central Park, Michel sees landscape as a territory that can be boldly structured and then left to be softened and corrupted by the local forces of nature and all using a palette of species that are entirely local and therefore thrive in their environment with minimum support.

Michel's response was ingeniously simple. Taking inspiration from wave forms sculpted in the sand, he imagined a sequence of erosion that could have formed this sandy bank to the lake. Together we proposed a series of interventions: a ha-ha along the road and an elevated section of ground to enclose the garage and form a shallow land bridge over an entrance into a beautiful glade of wild flowers that is open, through our building, to the lake beyond.

As to the design of the building, my thoughts turned to reinterpreting the traditional dacha. This we did by proposing an immensely heavy timber roof suspended off three large solid piers. These piers contained the services of the building, including a grand hearth. The great weight of the suspended overhanging timber roof and beams thus contrasted with the diaphanous glass enclosure.

*Opposite*
The dacha breaks the tree line and is the pivot between forest and lake.

*Overleaf*
The dacha is a refuge in the winter.

'Your brief to me is to create a building that will be beautiful, without ornament and inspired by the nature that surrounds it.

'When I design, I focus on how the building relates to its natural surroundings. The building will be beautiful because of how it sits in the landscape and most importantly how people enjoy it from the inside looking out.

'Your site has two incredible assets. First a potentially beautiful forest opening and second an incredible vista onto the lake. The forest aspects creates containment and the lake view is open and sublime.

'My response to your brief is to make our building the pivot between the forest and the lake. In this way you will be at the centre of this land-scape. I will design the building to bring the forest into the house and then open the house to the view.'

*Opposite*
The meadow rolls right up to the
glass walls of the dacha.

*The Butler Collection, Dorset, UK:* A private collection is a record of private passion. By the time I met the incisive Sir Michael Butler, parts of the collection had already been exhibited in Shanghai and at the V&A in London, both immense honours for an amateur collector. But the collection itself was housed in three garden sheds, and Butler's vision was to see it brought together into a permanent, didactic entity that could be handed on to his family in its best possible light. The building of a collector's gallery would realise a suitably prestigious setting for what is considered the world's most important collection of 17th-century Chinese porcelain. The project was thus driven by a passion that made Sir Michael a wonderful patron of architecture despite the strict economy of his budget.

We tried several potential sites in and around the garden, but in each case the relatively large building read far too dominantly. It is sometimes better and more effective to let the building find its natural setting and merge into its background. We eventually alighted on merging the gallery within an existing cluster of farmyard buildings. This proved appropriate to the site, and created a magical sequence of unexpected discovery that I suspect appealed to Sir Michael's wit.

The building was therefore conceived from the outside as a simple windowless agricultural barn and provided sensible building economies. On the inside, however, it delivers an unexpectedly grand gallery of substance and gravitas. Nine small galleries are arranged around a central nave. The design anticipates the collector spending hours in contemplation, rearranging pots to form new connections and considering new acquisitions. A long skylight brings natural light over a large study table where analysis and debate are focused. Each of the surrounding galleries contains sub-collections that are displayed on a curving sculptural dais.

Of all works of art, a collection of porcelain is surely the least demanding to house because it is not susceptible to UV, sunlight, temperature or humidity. The building is sealed, highly insulated, efficiently heated underfloor, and powered by a simple air-source heat pump. Lighting six hundred individual objects without creating a chaos of competing shadows is the real challenge. We settled on a practical system of translucent ceilings made of fabric stretched below light battens that generate a diffused 'north light' that casts minimal shadows but exposes the subtle colours of the pots.

*Opposite top*
The new building blends into the array of agricultural barns.

*Opposite bottom*
The concealed entrance to the Gallery creates a sense of expectation that turns to surprise.

*Overleaf*
The top-lit nave and its radiating galleries.

*Marsh House, Isle of Man*

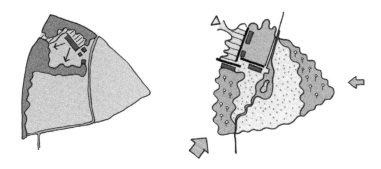

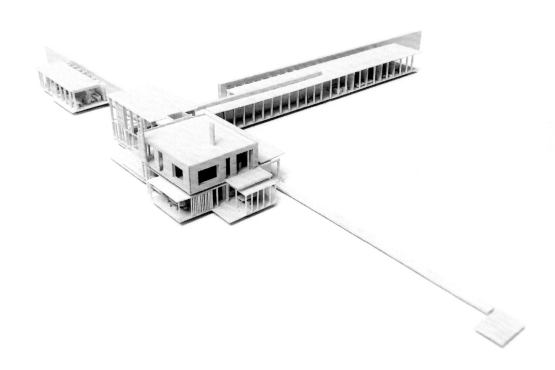

*Marsh House, Isle of Man:* All modern landscapes are to a greater or lesser extent de-naturalised by man. A project for an enlightened client moving to live and work on the wet and windswept Isle of Man provided the opportunity to rewild, and to explore ideas developed by great 18th-century landscape architects such as Capability Brown.

Farming and land ownership had transformed the territory into a series of independent geometric plots, one containing the house and two containing flat fields. A small stream diverted into a ditch defined the plots and traversed the site awkwardly at right angles. The existing house was huddled in a far corner, its back onto an embankment and its aspect over the fields to the sea beyond blanked off by a giant leylandii windbreak.

My aim was to move the owner from the edge of his land and place him at the heart of a newly naturalised landscape. I started by releasing the stream from the ditch to create a natural wetland with shallow earth structures that slow the flow of water and instigate a broad range of indigenous wetland flora and fauna.

I recalled advice from engineers that protection from the wind is often better achieved by deflecting and 'feathering' than by constructing impenetrable barriers that create unexpected eddies and downdrafts. I therefore set about analysing the prevailing winds and identifying lines of windbreaks that would protect the new location of the house for the key periods of the year. I proposed mass plantations of silver birch woods inspired by beautiful forests on the banks of Loch Rannoch in Scotland that I discovered were also native to the Isle of Man. Relative to private garden construction, agricultural mass plantation techniques are cheaper and generate faster growth.

At the centre of the composition, a small portion was then divided off from the rewilded landscape by two intersecting axial walls. The first, a long dry-stone wall, divides off the wetlands. The second defines an entrance courtyard on the roadside and on the other side a cloistered orchard onto the stream. At the apex of the composition and at the centre of the territory the house sat with its feet in the ponds.

The design set up a sequence of spaces from public to private that ended as a small pier. The project was therefore the intersection of man and nature; part human settlement, part wildlife sanctuary.

*Opposite top*
Diagrams showing the process of rewilding from agriculture to wildlife sanctuary.

*Opposite bottom*
The house and study are arranged along the axial wall facing the rewilded woods and water meadow. A second wall at right angles separates the entrance courtyard from the cloistered orchard.

*Overleaf*
The house places the owner at the heart of the rewilded landscape with its water meadows and silver birch windbreaks.

*El Mirador, Sotogrande*

_El Mirador, Sotogrande, Andalucia, Spain:_ In 2016 we were invited with six other architects from around the world to create designs for an undeveloped district of the Sotogrande resort in southern Spain. The client Marc Topiol, the CEO, intended to re-invent the art of resort living and asked us all to collaborate to develop the overall vision. Each of us was allocated a one-hectare site for a large, individual private house. Each response was markedly different. Our own site was at the top of the hill with views that stretched to Gibraltar and across the Alboran Sea to the North African Rif Mountains. The site had been untouched for centuries, and nature had imbedded itself precariously into the dry and rocky terrain, tenacious but fragile.

The process started with a presentation by the hugely charismatic Mediterranean landscape architect Jean Mus. Jean explained his concept for the park: a place where the historic flora and fauna could flourish, where barriers between plots would be concealed, where seasonal downpours would be harnessed and indigenous flora remain dominant. This contextual approach contrasted radically with the commercial norm of tightly clipped, over-watered lawns, with exotic plants from around the globe. Jean concluded his presentation by passing round essential oils made from local plants and herbs. The architects were left infused and inspired.

Our approach was to displace as little of the site as possible by inserting a series of encampment walls that enclosed an internal courtyard connected to a series of pavilions that were let into the hillside between the treasured existing trees.

As one enters the site from the land side, the sea view is hidden and unanticipated. The massive outer walls of the 'encampment', formed of rammed earth and clay from the site, sit in the uneven hillside like the walls of an abandoned ancient fort. You are corralled by the walls onto a gentle upwardly-sloping ramp that leads into the courtyard from where views of the distant landscape are subtly screened.

The courtyard, with its reflecting pools and textured walls, creates an unexpected stillness and snippets of vistas towards the open horizons. Beyond the water courtyard, four pavilions are separated from one another by open landscaped terraces with commanding views of the valley and out to sea. Communal life takes place from pavilion to pavilion across these landscaped courtyards that contain the ancient trees.

_Opposite top_
The massive rammed earth walls sit in the landscape like the ruins of an ancient fortress.

_Opposite bottom_
Snatched views through the entrance pavilion from the water court.

_Overleaf_
The daily life of the villa flows from pavilion to pavilion across landscaped terraces.

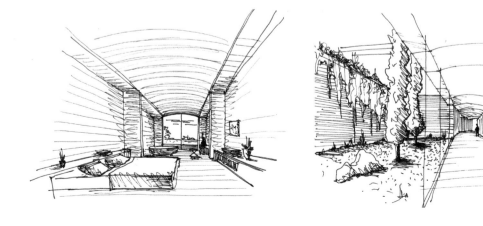

Below ground, in complete contrast to the bright, open life above, the spaces are cavernous with controlled light carefully cast from above onto hewn solid vertical surfaces. The bedrooms are formed as cave-like structures in cast-textured and coloured concretes. These open on to small, private, vaulted terraces and provide cool retreats from the blazing sun.

*Opposite top*
The pool area is organic in shape
to encourage people to nest.

*Opposite bottom*
The bedrooms and below-ground
areas are cave-like and private.

_Eyrie, Castletownshend, County Cork, Ireland:_ The clients were handing their large Irish home over to the next generation for summer vacations and had toyed with the idea of using an old coach house as their own summer home, away from their offspring's young families. Unlike the main house that sat grandly on a prominent lawn, the coach house was part of a walled service courtyard at the back of the site, perched perilously over a small inaccessible cove directly facing out to sea.

I was immediately attracted to develop a design that married this outward-looking drama with the comforting enclosure of its courtyard, to blend the two moods of the site into a single composition.

The courtyard was thus colonised as a private space for summer lunches among potted plants, protected from the wind and connected into the large living room that faced out to sea. The double-height living room looked out to the view through a glazed timber screen that was broken into comforting sections, with a banquette that lined the great window and made the entire space feel like a tree-house. A study and snug were located on the mezzanine and provided a vertiginous view over the living area and down to the cove below. The panelled bedroom was off the snug, a type of captain's cabin pointed directly out across Castle Haven and to the open sea beyond Horse Island.

_Opposite_
The eyrie sits perched on the
edge of the cliff facing out to sea.

*Heckfield Place, Hampshire*

*Heckfield Place, Hampshire, UK:* If confronted with a blank canvas, I'm dumbfounded. My architecture needs a site. So whenever I am asked what my dream commission would be, I tend to blank out because I see architecture as the process of exposing new dimensions to an existing place. Buildings can do this.

A commission for a spa and treatment centre, instigated by my long-time collaborator and friend Todd Longstaffe Gowan who was the landscape architect at Heckfield Place, presented an ideal challenge.

The estate and its grounds are listed, and extensive negotiations with the planners had already buttoned down all the potential sites. I started with a project for the walled gardens, but this proved to be a false start. I wandered around the extensive grounds, over towards the grand lake that was set within a noble forest of 200-year-old trees. At the far end the lake is dammed and sits about five metres above a small agricultural valley that drains the neighbouring fields. The lake discharges into a snaking brook that is unremarkable and unloved — it is constrained and functional.

I imagine a walk to the spa from the main building, through the woods, along the lake and down steps that follow a gentle water-fall that arrives into a secret valley. A small pond feeds the gently meandering brook. The building is roofed in plants and is visible only from its sinuous roof edge that mimics the sensual curves of the water course.

The curvilinear glass building is set a few stepping stones across the brook. Inside the building you are submerged in views of the intimate landscaped valley. Discreet shafts of light fall from tiny sky-lights set within the concrete roof. Rooms are circular, panelled in warm coloured timbers and arranged to engage the water's edge against the solid side of the valley wall. The space flows between these rooms as a river might flow between the rocks it has smoothed over time. The sounds of burbling water, rustling reeds and busy birdlife colour the atmosphere. At the far end of the building the treatment ends with a plunge into an invigorating natural pool that is set into a small landscaped creek.

Is it a building, is it a landscape?

*Opposite*
The new spa melts into the
reeded landscape of the brook.

# THE PAST IS A PRESENT

Embrace the future without
jettisoning the humanity, history
and colour of our past.

I learned a very great deal during my two decades in the Richard Rogers Partnership's creative hothouse, and perhaps nothing more important than during my third week when Richard pulled out images of Michelangelo's architectural work at the Piazza del Campidoglio. I had not an inkling that the high-tech Richard Rogers standing in front of me in a pink collarless shirt and ergonomic shoes was actively looking to the past to inspire his futurism. I had a lot to learn.

For 10,000 years humans made it their mission to formulate shelter wherever they settled. All our buildings are in one way or the other the offspring of those experiments and all are in different ways worthy of careful observation because they were refined from one generation to the next. To the observant, old buildings, from the largest monument to the smallest homesteads, provide a reserve of social and cultural ideas that might one day come in useful or provide inspiration. Old buildings also remind us that we are part of a long cultural continuum. They are a physical library of built ideas, a record of evolving experiments with habitat and representations of society and of the family. We have regularly erased our cultural past before recognising its proper value, just as we have applied this thoughtlessness to our natural environment. There is a cultural and environmental imperative for reworking the best of our old buildings and a long tradition of doing so in highly imaginative ways. Balance is required.

From the environmental engineering perspective alone, those buildings are important because they tended to use techniques that relied on resourcefulness to create comfort. Those pragmatic techniques of managing the environment have not suddenly become irrelevant. The bountiful availability of fossil fuel since the 1950s may have temporarily decoupled that intelligence from the making of modern buildings but, now that the chickens have come home to roost, increasing numbers of architects and engineers have progressively reconsidered and updated passive, age-old techniques that replace the energy-guzzling approach that was so wantonly and damagingly embraced.

I very much enjoy the challenge of working with old buildings. Like solving a complex riddle, the satisfaction in conservation projects comes when one has found a path through the maze of possibilities, and a 'new' understanding of the building is developed. Modification is usually, but not always, more resource-efficient than reconstruction. In the face of the acres of bland new developments that are colonising our cities, towns and villages, I am firmly in favour of conservation wherever it is feasible.

Despite what we are told, there is no right or wrong way to restore a building. Some of our greatest buildings, like Notre Dame de Paris and Westminster Abbey, are the result of centuries of accumulated design and reconstruction. Others, like the Taj Mahal in Agra and the Twin Towers in New York, were built as designed. Others still were built as designed and have undergone multiple modifications from the day they were completed. The need to replace the Twin Towers triggered a national debate, and the need to restore the Cathedral of Notre Dame has already sparked fierce argument between those who want it restored to its former design and those who see the fire as an opportunity to express the spirit of the current age with a contemporary interpretation of its soaring vaults and spire. These major projects demand serious consideration, but so too in a lesser way do the smaller and far more numerous projects that abound in our older cities.

There are better and worse ways of restoring and reusing old buildings, and only subjective ways of judging right from wrong. It is therefore, like any other architectural venture, a highly innovative practice. It is fortunate that most key historic buildings in Europe and whole swathes of land are protected under conservation laws. Reuse is however closely controlled by the conservation fashion of the day and risks being applied with a stultifying inflexibility that can exclude invention. From a design perspective, the challenge is to judge what level of deference to grant the original structure or author, and always to decide how to express the continuum of past and present.

Michelangelo's work at the Campidoglio shows how free he was with the reuse of old buildings. It might look like a pure construction, but it is actually a highly pragmatic reinvention of a cluster of medieval buildings that created a spectacular leap forward for Renaissance architecture and place-making.

Modernist architects are once again working in increasingly creative ways with old buildings and evolving a deeper and more flexible exploration of the continuum with our past. I see this as an evolution of the Modernist philosophy that is greatly to society's advantage.

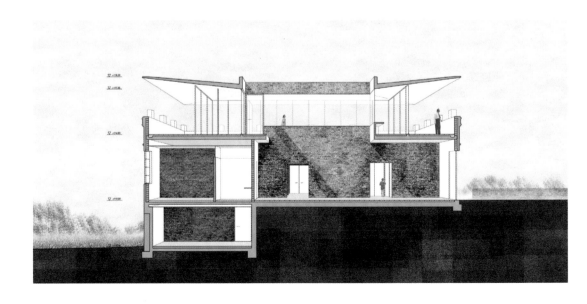

*The Fort, Girona, Spain:* A commission to refurbish a 19th-century farmhouse on the crest of a hill provided an opportunity to reinvigorate an old structure. The building was a proud, simple statement perched above a town, with the Pyrenees as a distant but powerful backdrop lining the horizon. The building seemed to know what it was and that it alone commanded its territory.

It was, however, old and tattered and in need of total restoration. These 19th-century farmhouses were predicated on a way of life and a type of formality that were not relevant to the current owners, who wanted to structure the renovation around a new and highly convivial lifestyle that could be sustained throughout the seasons, not just during the summer months.

The bones of the house enclosed a central open courtyard that contained the stairway to the roof. The manipulation of this courtyard became the heart of a redevelopment strategy that allowed the house to breathe in the summer and hunker down in the winter.

The courtyard became the centre of life in the house, except now it could be shaded in summer and by degree closed when the weather was becoming intemperate in winter. The communal rooms opened to the courtyard and could benefit from the cool air that was naturally conditioned by the shaded stone space.

From the rooftop, the house enjoyed a 360-degree panoramic view from the mountains to the town it dominated. But in the summer the roof was exposed to the blazing sun, and this militated against its use. Together with Chris Wise of Expedition Engineering, we introduced a roof that hovered to the edge of the old building, suspended on the glazing itself. This created a 360-degree horizontal strip that framed the view and when gently lit from below created a glowing crown as seen from the town below and across the land.

*Previous*
Piranesi engraving of the Piazza Campidoglio on the Capitoline Hill, Rome.

*Opposite top*
The glowing roof creates a hovering crown over the building.

*Opposite bottom*
The new roof is suspended on the glass façade and frames 360-degree panoramic views of the landscape and mountains beyond.

*Echo House, Dublin*

*Echo House, Dublin, Ireland:* In 2005 we were approached to design a house in Dublin for a heart surgeon on a prominent spit of land within sight of the Martello Tower immortalised by James Joyce in *Ulysses.*

The site contained an original neo-Georgian building that had been doubled in size and degraded by an array of haphazard extensions. The architecture of the building was not considered to be of heritage interest. However, from the nearby Bullock Harbour and for passing sailors it was a well-loved landmark, and the word-of-mouth assumption that it had housed the harbour master further characterised the building. Thus it was a cultural landmark and a physical beacon, whose loss would have been regretted by the community.

Our solution was to conserve the landmark character of the structure but to conceive a thoroughly new house made up of two equivalent but complementary parts. All the extensions were demolished and the old façades restored to their original form. The extensions were replaced with a new concrete structure that echoed the proportions of the original villa and joined by the equivalent of an architectural hyphen — a glass link.

This set up an intriguing formal and intellectual dialogue between old and new. The old was restored with traditional materials and details, the new wing was thoroughly contemporary in its conception, in its use of concrete and glass and its corresponding detailing, and both were heated by a highly efficient ground source heating system.

The composition gave equal weight to both parts. Together they carried the history of the site and projected a statement of the present, creating a composition that was to our mind greater than the sum of its parts. There is certainly nothing 'pure' or 'honest' in this approach. It represents an attempt to create the new, whilst reconciling the community's desire for continuity.

*Opposite top*
The landmark quality of the original building is retained for sailors.

*Opposite bottom*
Echo House juxtaposes the old with the new in a balanced composition of equals.

_Edwin Lutyens at Piccadilly, London, UK:_ In 2002 I was invited by architect and friend Annabelle Selldorf to collaborate on the conversion of the famous Lutyens-designed Midland Bank into a flagship for the avant-garde Hauser & Wirth Gallery. This was their first London venture and they chose a non 'white cube' space to launch their arrival onto the scene.

Lutyens had deliberately eschewed Modernism and taken his cue from the neighbouring St James's Church by Sir Christopher Wren. His 1922 building was conceived as a highly florid version of Wren's 17th-century architectural style. That new style was dubbed 'Wren-aissance' and was lauded and vilified in equal measure by rival architectural critics. Consecutive office workers had brutally integrated modern banking requirements with no consideration for the interiors and with damaging results. The building's Grade 2* listing now afforded the same protection to the new abominations as to Lutyens's original work.

Our approach was forensic. We began by carefully stripping out the additions made over many decades until we could properly ascertain the shapes of the original rooms and the scope required to repair, replace or re-invent missing elements. Then we sought to integrate the Gallery's requirements for flexible lighting, power and data and establish structural positions for hanging and suspending paintings and substantial sculptures without damaging the protected panelling or overloading the existing structures.

Hauser & Wirth are extremely popular amongst artists because they are prepared to push the boat out for every exhibition. In practice, the space must have the capability of being quickly and efficiently transformed in thoroughly unexpected ways to suit artists as distinct as Louise Bourgeois and Paul McCarthy, who shot his outrageous video 'Piccadilly Circus' in the building before the restoration had begun.

We evolved modifications based on Lutyens's designs to subtly shift the design towards its new gallery use. Our hand was light even though the amount of amendment was sizeable. The conversion extended the life of the building which is currently occupied by the prestigious Maison Assouline.

_Opposite top_
Lutyens's 1922 building on Piccadilly.

_Opposite bottom_
Sculptures by Berlinde De Bruyckere contrasted against the rich panelling of the new Hauser & Wirth contemporary art gallery.

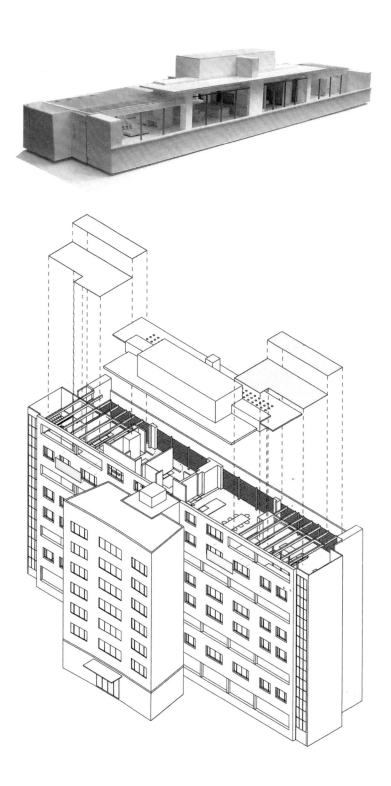

*Wells Coates at 10 Palace Gate, Kensington, London, UK:* Wells Coates was a generation younger than Lutyens and a leading pioneer of British Modernism. 10 Palace Gate was initiated only twelve years after Lutyens's work at Piccadilly and highlights the broad range of architectural thinking that characterised the pre-WW2 period with obvious resonances with our contemporary world.

At 10 Palace Gate, he had explored radical ways of conceiving and constructing an urban apartment block, including pioneering the use of new materials and building techniques — an innovative approach that would be rare today despite the huge appetite amongst the young for new ways of living. Wells Coates had designed the top floor to contain the porter's flat within a large, Mediterranean-styled terrace spanned by concrete pergolas. The vagaries of the British climate conspired to limit the use of the terrace, and we were commissioned to seek permission to enclose the terrace and create a large penthouse.

No obvious precedent existed to steer our design, but we took our cue from how Wells Coates embraced modern technologies and materials. Like many of his contemporaries, he was inspired by the cruise ship and the precision and delicacy of yacht design. In so many cases of conservation, the finesse of an old building is lost when past craftmanship is replaced with better performing modern systems that tend to be heavier and bulkier.

Our approach was to develop a roof system of triple-glazed sky-lights that sat over the pergola with its frames hidden by the beams themselves. Insulated timber shutters between the concrete beams could be opened or closed to control the daylight and the sense of enclosure, thus allowing conditions in the penthouse to be altered depending on weather conditions. The design conserved the look of the original façade with its slotted cruise-ship openings and perforated pergola roof, but delivered a highly insulated new glass-enclosed space. This careful approach was carried through with the further additions designed to add taller elements under a new concrete canopy perforated with glass bricks. All details were kept as slim and lightweight as possible.

We inhabited Wells Coates's design philosophy and aesthetic, embraced the opportunities of contemporary technologies, and created a thoroughly modern wrapping without unbalancing the overall composition or altering the substance of his vision.

*Opposite top*
The new penthouse with its glazed roof and canopied main space reflect contemporary detailing inspired by yacht design.

*Opposite bottom*
The new glass and concrete roof forms a new skyline for the pioneering 1930s' apartment building.

_Richard Rogers at Wimbledon, London, UK:_ In 2010, the Richard Rogers Charity gifted the iconic but tired Wimbledon House to Harvard Graduate School of Design. The building had been listed among the top five per cent of protected buildings in the country. The intention was that the house be restored and converted for use by a new Fellowship Programme specifically aimed at researching The City. There would be two resident Fellows at any one time and regular events and symposiums.

This kind of restoration and conversion work is painstaking, fraught with difficult negotiations with heritage bodies and unlike most listed buildings the architect was alive to comment on how I was doing. So when Richard formally asked me to join the shortlist that Harvard were drawing up for the work I was quite reluctant. It turned out that the process of refurbishing the Grade 2*-listed 1968 steel and glass house proved far more interesting than I could possibly have imagined.

I had known the building since the 1980s and had never seen a domestic space like it. Open plan, fully glazed onto the gardens, bathrooms with glass ceilings, sliding partitions for walls and thoroughly humanised by Richard's calm, cultured, Modernist parents. All sunlight, pottery, yellow blinds and plants.

I assumed that this modern building was exactly as drawn, but it soon became clear that the house had undergone several iterations and changes, even by 1980. The following 25 years were no different. I had initially set myself the challenge of recapturing the spirit and clarity of vision from those early years, but as with all restoration projects we had to establish which of its many pasts were the most historically important or relevant. We delved into old drawings to decide what to keep and what to replace and how to accommodate the changes required by Harvard.

Once we started analysing the building it became apparent that it had been a living experiment and was not the fixed and complete building that I had imagined. This posed further restoration dilemmas. Most often with protected buildings (and especially masonry ones) it is the fabric and workmanship that are of great heritage interest. In this case, Richard had been prototyping the idea of a home constructed from a kit of parts, of which only the bones were truly permanent. The rest — that included in this case the minimally thin two-inch PVC-clad insulating external walls, the double-glazed gable walls, and the roofs — were designed with specific lifespans after

_Opposite_
The yellow steel portal frames mark an enfilade of open and enclosed spaces that run from courtyard to garden.

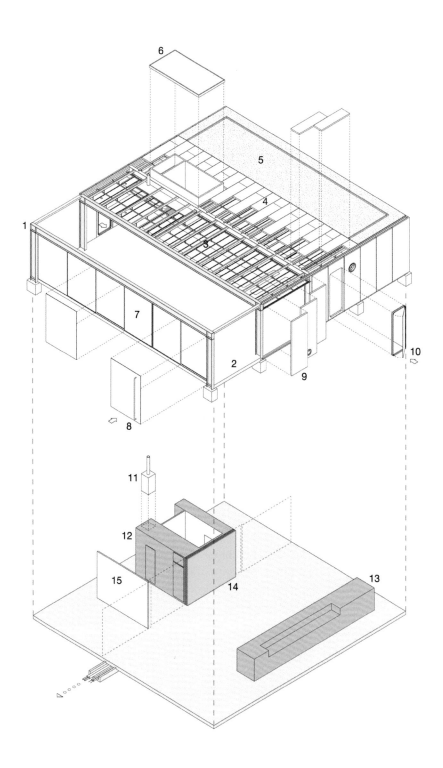

which they were to be replaced with whatever new materials had been dreamt up in the intervening period. In practice this meant that the asbestos panels needed replacement with non-toxic fire board and the 1990s' roof insulation was replaced with better-performing vacuum insulation (expensive bubble wrap) and covered in a new membrane. Remarkably, most of the 1968 oversized double-glazed gable walls survived 50 years, some 20 years longer than their advertised lifespan and did not require replacement. Achieving the overall renovation and conversion required rebuilding 75 per cent of the envelope of the building.

Richard's design had anticipated that new and better-performing materials would be developed and had embraced the idea of updating the parts with contemporary materials and technologies. Ironically the building fabric was now protected by law. This led to some interesting conversations with the heritage bodies. Eventually Historic England, Merton Council and the Twentieth Century Society came around to the idea that the introduction of elements that increased the performance of the building was acceptable as long as we retained the aesthetics of the original. We used the early design drawings and our 'eye' to ensure that the proportions and key details were safeguarded or reinterpreted.

Wimbledon House is as clear a diagram for a building as Richard ever produced. A series of steel portal frames arranged on a regular grid that could theoretically be added to or taken away. These structures were used to enclose two buildings. Separating them from the road is a landscaped mound. Separating them from each other is a landscaped courtyard and then the rear garden. The house and garden were a total design, an amazing fusion of interior and exterior spaces, an enfilade of open and enclosed spaces. The restoration or re-invention of the garden therefore presented both a challenge and an opportunity. Working once again with Todd Longstaffe-Gowan we developed a new garden that rationalised the way the building would be used by the Fellows and the visiting public. We used planting to gently screen the Fellows' accommodation whilst keeping the views into the courtyard and gardens.

The final building is a painstaking reapplication of the concept replete with careful protection of original patina, along with the evidence of the early problems and their rectification. It is a new building in a new context but from a didactic and emotional perspective nothing has been lost of the original vision.

*Opposite*
The building is conceived as a kit of parts that can be assembled and modified into different shapes and sizes. The restoration project included re-engineering the individual components, utilising new materials whilst conserving the patina and aesthetic of the original building.

*Overleaf*
The ceilings are restored replete with the original radiant heating and 1960s' replica light fittings. The mirrored bedroom is divided by carefully restored sliding green doors. Views extend through the courtyard towards the Fellows' building.

*Villa, Glebe Place*

*Villa, Glebe Place, London, UK:* Working in a historic city is a little like working with an old building but on a larger scale. For me the task is to integrate the new without compromising the character of the old. The purpose is to recalibrate the totality towards a new future.

In the 19th century, Chelsea was a popular, affordable part of London where artists built themselves studio homes. Unlike the buildings in many neighbouring streets, those on Glebe Place are experiments with different styles of architecture. The character of the place resonates with variety and artistry.

In the midst of these studios the Edwardians built a large modern school that was abandoned and up for residential redevelopment. By the time our clients purchased the site the project had already delivered a special needs school as their community contribution. We were invited to compete for the commission to design two large new houses in the playground that links Glebe Place to Old Church Street. The sites bordered Grade 1 and Grade 2 buildings, which in other words required great sensitivity.

Glebe Place has become a very desirable area largely because the street is relatively small in scale, but the buildings are all very different and enjoy double-height artist studios and large windows. This was the simple cue for our proposed design for the house that sat deep within the school site against an unbecoming large brick wall. Our key concern was to not upset the delicate scale of the street. By analysing those existing buildings and views along Glebe Place as the passer-by would approach our site, we began to develop a scheme that would act as a focal point that extended the street into the site.

The new building is much larger than its typical 19th-century neighbours and as large again below ground. We therefore subdivided the above-ground building into two parts separated by a staircase that gives the occupants the feeling of ascending and descending within the canopy of the large London plane tree that stands in its garden. The design is of a scale that matches that of Glebe Place, to which it presents a simple stone façade with a dominant vertical window. The window echoes vertical features on some of the neighbouring buildings. The private bedroom wing is clad in a dark recessive bronze and seemingly disappears from view.

The tall thin window draws the eye of the passer-by deep into the site. The new façade is then decorated with an irregular grid of cross-cut travertine. The effect is of a highly textured façade that is graphically bold from a distance but grows in complexity, texture and

*Opposite top*
The building is visually divided to reduce its scale to that of Glebe Place. The long vertical window picks up on local details in the street.

*Opposite bottom*
The vertical window offers a strong graphic that leads the eye and extends Glebe Place into the site.

*Overleaf*
The building's surface is highly decorated with natural patterns created by cross-cutting the travertine stonework. Openable, perforated screens cast dappled light into the double-height drawing-room.

*Villa, Glebe Place*

ornament as it is approached. I had in mind the façade of the Palazzo Dario on the Grand Canal, with its marbled surfaces and deeply recessed windows. These decorative devices aim to bed this modern building into its historic site.

The ground floor is designed with each internal space flowing into an associated landscaped area designed by Tom Stuart-Smith. In this way the ground floor appears to occupy the entire site, and in the temperate seasons family life naturally spreads out into the courtyards.

Above this garden level and located behind the Glebe Place façade is a dramatic double-height formal drawing-room and galleried study that faces south over the beautiful new gardens.

This façade is screened with openable perforated louvres that provide solar shade, that dapple the sunlight and give less or more privacy. This is a grand room for a contemporary 'salon', a social meeting place that it is hoped will continue the tradition and culture of debate and intellectual rivalry that has characterised the street since the 19th century.

*Opposite*
The double-height south-facing drawing-room can be opened to the view or screened for privacy and solar control.

*William Chambers at Wick House, Richmond Hill, London, UK:* Wick House exemplifies the discussion of this chapter and maybe takes the idea of the re-invention of history to its limit. In 1768 Sir William Chambers completed a house for Sir Joshua Reynolds on Richmond Hill. We understand that Reynolds used the house as a venue for dinner parties and as a painting studio. We know that the design was altered during construction to include a bow window, the very same window from which Reynolds painted his famous scene of the Thames across Petersham Meadows. We also know that Reynolds was quite displeased when Chambers increased his agreed fee to cover the amendment: *plus ça change*.

Within 30 years an additional level was added; within 100 years there was a total Victorian makeover, including a new wing, endless external ornamentation and complete remodelling of the interiors. Then within 200 years the building was stripped back again to receive a further total makeover, this time Neo-Georgian in style, for its conversion into a nurses' boarding hostel.

The building is prominent on Richmond Hill, is listed, and is surrounded by protected and listed buildings in a predominantly Georgian style. It faces a view protected in 1902 by Act of Parliament. The building is in poor condition and we were commissioned to turn it back into a single-family dwelling. Which iteration of its history do we have recourse to? What is the cultural importance of this site to the future? What is the honest thing to do?

On the face of it, restoring the building to the shape it was when it was listed would seem the logical and legal heritage requirement, especially given the extremely informed neighbours and local heritage societies. However, this would have restored what Chambers scholar John Harris considered its worst possible iteration. Returning it to its Victorian manifestation, replete with balconies, conservatories and decoration would reintroduce a Victorian flourish to the primarily Georgian context. Returning it to its original 18th-century state would require reducing its height and demolishing the large and domineering wing built by the Victorians, thereby reducing its size and value, a very unpromising commercial proposition. Meanwhile the building was decaying fast and on the government's buildings-at-risk list.

John Harris remained adamant that the key heritage moment was the meeting of the two giants of late 18th-century British culture and therefore any restoration work should see that moment enshrined.

*Opposite top*
The building in 2019. The projecting Victorian Wing to the left and the main Chambers' structure to the right were all given a radical neo-Georgian make-over in the 1940's.

*Opposite middle*
Wick House in the 1790's

*Opposite bottom*
Aerial view of the Victorian makeover, replete with new wing and smoking tower, rooftop mansards, south-facing verandas and multiple embellishments.

*William Chambers at Wick House*

The building forms a pair with a contemporaneous neighbour. At first we explored borrowing details from that very elegant building until another eminent historian, Paul Velluet, sourced an early drawing that proved to us that the original Chambers design was quite austere and in stark contrast to its neighbour. I consider that despite Reynolds's success and fame, his wealth was not extensive and the budget for a building for his occasional entertaining and work was possibly quite modest (the land having been gifted to him). Chambers, who was himself at the time involved in far grander projects, may even have passed the project on to a younger architect within his office. As a result the building appears to be quite modest, save for the artist studio with its bow window.

Our proposal began, in deference to John Harris, with reinstating a large, double-height artist studio space directly off the ground floor hall facing the famous view. This creates a new centre of gravity for the house from which all activities radiate. A new 'library stair' connects to the kitchen-dining areas below and the study and guest suite above, through the studio. Circulation between these key social areas engages the famous view.

Our proposal lies in restoring the austere Georgian façade, reinterpreting its internal organisation around a dominant artist studio, and then entirely replacing the Victorian wing with a more recessive modern structure than the existing edifice.

If the Chambers structure is to dominate, then the replacement wing must neither compete with it nor be seen to extend it. We have designed a perforate, layered façade of terracotta louvres and glass that is akin to a large conservatory. In this way we intend it to be complementary but not read as part of the Chambers building. The two neighbouring 18th-century buildings are thus paired and bookended with conservatory-like structures.

The vertical terracotta louvres of the new wing are manufactured in a similar tone to the original Chambers brickwork. Together the two structures from entirely different periods make a fully functioning modern house.

They say 'history is written by the victors' and buildings are no exception to this process. Whole swathes of buildings by previous cultures have been demolished, removed and made to disappear in the name of 'cleansing' history, of reinforcing ethnic claims or underpinning contemporary doctrines. Some architects by contrast seek to conserve as much of a building's history as possible in order to reveal

*Opposite top*
Drawing from the early 1800s showing the relationship between 'Wick House' and the more refined and decorated 'The Wick'.

*Opposite bottom*
The proposal restores the original austere Chambers façade and replaces the Victorian wing with a new recessive contemporary wing. The masonry buildings appear balanced and are bookended by their conservatory-like structures.

the fluidity and complexity of its past. This approach is exemplified in David Chipperfield's masterpiece at the Neues Museum in Berlin. There is an important moral dimension to playing with our past, and vigilance and cool judgement are essential.

At Wick House we have referenced elements from the building's own past, I hope benignly. Our design celebrates what is considered to be the most significant moment in its history. This conservation is a re-invention but, quite unusually, the broad consensus of experts, planners and historians consider it an appropriate solution to the conundrum of the site. After 10 years of neglect and decay, that consensus will unlock the private funding for a restoration that will ensure the meeting of these great figures of the 18th century will be celebrated and preserved for the future.

*Opposite*
The new south-facing façade expresses the reintroduced artist studio and its verandas. The transparency of the new wing is designed to leave the historic masonry building as the dominant feature.

# IT'S ALL IN THE DETAIL

The touchstone of a work of architecture
is the manner in which it is realised.

The touchstone of a work of architecture is the manner in which it is realised, how the materials feel to the touch and react to the light — literally. Like the score of a symphony in which every note, chord or movement is tirelessly considered, altered, balanced until the first day it is performed, so too the architect must endlessly balance the constraints and opportunities that emerge during the gestation period of a project down to the smallest detail and often right up until the moment it is being constructed on site. I have been fortunate to have had demanding clients who expect quality even on a low budget. These clients have understood the process and have provided the level of commitment needed to design down to the smallest detail.

The great public and private buildings with which we are all familiar bear witness to the extraordinary care and invention that have been applied. The architectural giants of the 20th century were just as careful as the great artisans of our fine traditional buildings, and instilled their innovative work with a sensibility and invention that continue to delight. It is this detailed work that provides templates which inspire others and eventually inform massproduction. But there is no shortcut between concept and realisation — it requires single-mindededness, blood, sweat and tears.

Choice of material and handling of minute details and junctions can, for example, make the difference between a building reading as tiles applied to a structure or as a solid imposing form. Choice of textures and colours will determine whether a building fuses into its context or stands apart. Whilst either approach can be appropriate, the final effect cannot be left to chance by passing it on to others.

For the last century, buildings have been increasingly mass-produced and more recently made of components assembled by robots or printed by high-tech machines. But buildings will still be inhabited by people, touched by the hand, and are still subject to our primeval human sensitivities and needs.

My own preference is to deliver the appearance of hand-crafted buildings even if they are made of industrial materials and assembled from factory-made products. Even futuristic buildings can continue the age-old sense of belonging to the land. More and more new recycled materials will be produced from waste or from base materials to reduce embodied energy or to protect rare stocks. We need architects to constantly explore and develop new aesthetic ways of handling these materials.

Curiously it is now very common worldwide to diminish the role of the instigating architects and distance them from the task of translating their own ideas into reality. The argument, simply put, is that those 'conceptual' architects are too precious, unworldly or expensive to be trusted to see their concept through to its conclusion.

In the past, local authorities in the UK had their own architectural departments and therefore took immense pride in the quality of the detail of their public buildings. In the 1980s it was decided to cut the cost of public works by passing responsibility on to commercial contractors to design and build those buildings more cheaply. For the most part this led to many local authority architects' departments simply fading away. Commercial providers of public buildings are generally constrained to reduce the amount of design time on projects and particularly on developing detail. The result of this approach has spawned the idea that public works can be second-rate and, with some notable exceptions, bland public environments are now widespread. Contemporary society is losing out a great deal from this approach.

In my time as Chair of the RIBA Awards group, my colleagues and I judged the very top public and private buildings in the country, some 400 out of the hundreds of thousands that are built annually in the UK. Even among this elite group of buildings, good architectural concepts consistently failed to achieve their potential because the manner in which the building was brought to life lacked the finesse to deliver the spirit of the concept. The result is fewer characterful buildings, and users who are less inspired by their environments.

By contrast, philanthropist Paul Hamlyn, while Chancellor of the poorest university in the country, donated the fees for Richard Rogers Partnership to design a standard cost university building that was about to be constructed. Hamlyn insisted that Rogers designed from the concept to the detail, and the building subsequently won multiple awards and became the iconic flagship of the university.

Along with many of my colleagues, I have taken on public commissions with standard construction budgets to demonstrate the extra that can be generated by applying the same level of design input from concept to detail that might be expected by an exigent private client. In numerous cases this has delivered award-winning buildings of substantially greater quality than the norm. These public buildings make greater impact and deliver inspiring environments that in return are greatly respected by their users. This is simply because the architect has given the design process more time, care and attention.

Good design from concept to detail delivers greater permanent quality. More public or private philanthropy of Paul Hamlyn's type would see a marked improvement in the quality of our public buildings for the benefit of all.

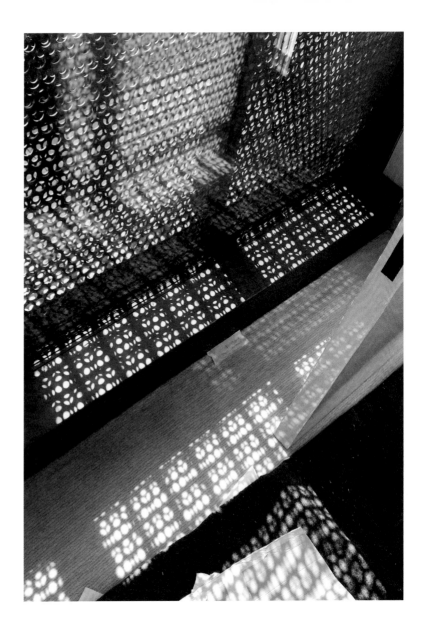

p80   Think Tank and jetty
p82   Marylebone School
      external stair
p83   Marylebone School
      internal stair
p84   Talisman fireplace/door/
      bookcase divider
p85   Talisman enfilade
p86   Artist's House floating
      staircase
p87   The Mount felt walls and
      translucent drapes
p88   Richmond Hill atrium
p89   Artist's House study
p90   Artist's house kitchen
p91   Light house detail
p92   Mews house enfilade
p93   Mews house stair
p94   Old Church Street exterior
      louvres
p95   Old Church Street interior
      light effect
p96   Film Den interior glass
      corner
p97   Film Den glass exterior
      glass corner
p98   The Mount enfilade
p99   Music practice room,
      Marylebone School
p100  Mews house stair
p101  Richmond Hill twisting
      stair

# HOME IS WHERE THE HEARTH IS

Housing must satisfy both
conscious and subconscious needs.

Not so long ago, families really did share their homes. The equivalent homesteads across the globe generally had a central hearth where the cooking took place and people congregated for warmth and to socialise. Sleeping was around the periphery. The luxury of having your own bedroom came relatively recently for the majority in the UK but is now considered a basic standard. This luxury has been replaced by the luxury of having your own bathroom, which is now the norm for much housing development. As wealth increases, so ever more 'luxury' is creating ever more separation within the home, within the family unit and between neighbours.

Housing must satisfy both conscious and subconscious needs and both internal and external relationships. It is a complex task, and in this context the assumption against involving architects to innovate and shape our public housing is a dangerously false economy. No doubt the rejection of this approach has been justified by the residual aversion to the image and poor management of the brutalist public housing projects foisted on citizens during the 1960s and 1970s. In reality, I suspect, it is simply because initial costs are greater, and these are not considered over the long life of the building. Successive UK governments have ducked the public housing issue and continue to promote the notion that it should be left to the market to sort out. The requirement on developers to provide free affordable housing with every development is not providing what we need and is a tax on development by another name. The intentions might be good but in recent years they have been successfully circumvented for reasons of profitability or feasibility.

The housing crisis is upon us in the UK and the problem with crisis management is the speed with which resolution must be delivered. UK governments are now used to delegating these responsibilities to the market, and the market in turn prefers to roll out existing solutions rather than to innovate. Large projects are simpler to control in terms of planning and simpler to mass-produce; existing templates are easier to roll out than multiples of smaller bespoke or innovative 'pocket' projects. Most importantly, the large projects deliver the bland large headline figures that politicians are looking for. This might suit administrative processes, but it hardly solves the problem of revitalising our quirky village centres, our characterful town centres or our deprived inner cities or promotes the exploration of better solutions. These places can provide vast numbers of high-quality homes that will actually revive the life of communities and attractiveness of town centres but require smaller, more agile, more carefully considered architectural solutions, housing that is woven into the fabric of the place and brings communities together. And let us not forget accommodating the elderly within our communities, down the road from their families, so that they become once more part of the everyday landscape of our children's lives.

In my time as an RIBA judge, we awarded the work of housing providers who delivered high quality new communities within the standard financial constraints. But the number of those exemplary housing projects pale into insignificance by comparison to the volumes of bland housing delivered by the market. For a first world nation whose government auditors are more than capable of calculating real, long term value there is no excuse.

There is an abundance of skilful architects available to deliver characterful pockets of housing on multiple gap sites that would consolidate communities in our cities, towns and villages. These types of housing also better suit the needs of our younger generations that are starting off on in life with new social and spatial requirements and are happy to re-engage with age-old sensible ideas such as shared facilities and co-housing projects. Moreover, mass production and new construction techniques need to be designed into the process of delivering these homes. Innovation is a constant need.

There is a growing consensus towards a more honest way for paying for public housing or in the alternative for incentives that reward higher-quality housing or, dare I say it, quite simply for direct public procurement of long-lasting public housing designed by good architects. By not building quality housing we are dumbing down our future built legacy, constraining family life, reducing well-being and driving our children onto their screens or onto the streets where they can find release from the utterly banal.

And yet we have only to look to the UK's heritage of public housing projects or to flagship contemporary projects to find ample blueprints of successful high-density housing; types of housing that will continue to delight and perform for old and young, rich and poor residents and will do so for years to come.

I am therefore advocating taking housing seriously once again and reinstituting direct public patronage to design the volumes of public homes that the government is so desperate to provide but in their desperation are likely to deliver without due consideration to real long-term quality. This would require a new generation of nimble planners and civil servants to encourage and deliver such a nationwide programme. Further investment in our planning system and financial incentives are needed to produce high-quality public housing with convivial public spaces. Such public philanthropy would repurpose our profession and steer our work towards delivering greater public good.

The architect's home is the perfect test-bed for design ideas — it is a mini-laboratory for experiment and prototyping. I have been at the same address for over 25 years and the one constant has been change, often much to my partner's dismay. The requirements of being single, then working from home, then adding a lover, then locating my studio and assistants at home, then moving the studio and assistants out and gaining a family has required fundamental changes in the amount of space required and the way the space has been used.

Fortunately, we were able to expand by linking up to the one-bed apartment next door to create a family-sized unit. Not rocket science but an important principle that has been used for decades in continental apartment blocks but is difficult to achieve in the UK for technical and legal reasons. This type of common-sense solution should increasingly inform the design of new apartment buildings with units that can expand and contract laterally without the high environmental, financial and time costs involved in converting the traditional UK building.

The current iteration of my home is littered with design and furniture ideas that I have tested and then developed further for private projects. Creating the 'bespoke', a design that departs from the standard, is an expensive option and is generally the privilege of the wealthy. Design is time-consuming and a 'luxury' unless the number of homes being built is sufficient to gain from economies of scale. The key to sharing the benefits of high-quality design is marrying innovative design with modern manufacturing technologies. If the specific design has the capability of being manufactured in different materials, finishes or dimensions then this offers a great range of variety. If that works, then the additional design time required to do a good job becomes affordable.

Private housing is a great research ground for new architectural and interior details, be it the design of the kitchen, cupboards, bookshelves, windows, wall finishes, floors or doors. Sounds strange but manufacturing usually follows in the footsteps of bespoke design and those designs are today usually conceived for private clients and varied for the broader market. Private patronage is still important in the whole scheme of things, and often the best ideas emerge in their fledgling state when the architects are in their passionate infancy and care about the smallest minute detail as if their lives depended on it.

Our contemporary technologies and the design of our homes are not teaching new generations to compromise and to share but

Previous
The Japanese hearth.

Opposite
Our home is the result up of years of piecemeal experiments with layout, surfaces, lighting, furniture and joinery.

to actually shun physical proximity and mutual respect. We are being nudged ever further towards the dubious rewards of total independence. Separation is now entirely accepted as the appropriate organisation of a house and belies millennia of experience where most people lived in much closer and, you might argue, more annoying proximity to one another. Separation in the modern domestic scenario means corridors and enclosure. Keeping your voice down to not annoy the rest of the family is obsolete. We can be as selfish as we like.

My own work tries to push back in favour of encouraging social interaction wherever possible. I do this by maximising the importance of communal rooms, by minimising the use of corridors, by introducing split levels to create volume and by flowing spaces into each other. It means we are constrained to think about others. It means we are living in each other's worlds and know what is going on. It also means we all get to share the best views and spaces.

Good architecture, from the design of the home to the apartment block or to the street, can nudge people into closer social contact with each other but we all need the skills to cope. In my view those skills are learnt at home and passed on, which is why the design of the home remains so critical.

In my own flat we decided to only have one communal living space and we've placed the kitchen bang in the middle of it which works very well for us. We congregate around the kitchen island, which although made from cool stainless steel is slightly warmed by its outdated, inefficient, golden incandescent lighting, a happy accident that seems to recreate the look and feel of a traditional hearth, and friends comment on this positively. Getting people away from this 'hearth' to sit on the sofa is almost impossible. A deep psychological glue seems to fix them to this spot.

The position of the kitchen in the centre of the room means that everything else can change depending on what is going on. Then by keeping the bedrooms tiny, by eliminating corridors, by limiting the number of bathrooms and by always prioritising communal space we have created a sense of spatial luxury and community that belies the actual size of the unit.

My clients are not buying my style, they are asking me to design a spatial organisation tailored to their particular needs. No matter the size of the house that I am commissioned to design, I always seek to engender conviviality, to keep the interconnectivity of spaces, to ensure that people move through, around or in view of shared spaces

*Opposite*
The kitchen island is at the centre of the apartment and is the heart of home life. People congregate there as if pinned to the spot.

so that they remain constantly present and part of the experience of the home.

Light is a constant obsession. I love sunlight and track its movement across all rooms in the house, trying to seize it where I can, trying to play with its shadows and envisaging how it will change the mood of the room during the day and across the seasons. I try to introduce natural daylight and drill it into the darkest recesses of the house. As the room gets darker, your eyes adjust and even a minimal amount of daylight has a positive impact on the quality of that space. At night time I use warm artificial light to turn the house in on itself. I try to recreate the imagined warmth and colour of a yesteryear home and create a sense of calm, repose and security.

In both the country and the city I am obsessed with the view out of the window. In my tiny Dorset cottage I have tested timber windows that frame views into the forest or out across fields to distant hills or from the bed frame the moonlit sky or scudding clouds in the dawn light. Even if the property is looking at a blank wall a metre away, I will introduce plants. If we are lucky enough to have a garden, then I will work with a landscape architect to create a stunning backdrop of plants to the internal rooms. I have always enjoyed working with Todd Longstaffe-Gowan because he treats my disciplined lines with a gardener's irreverence, brings a historian's understanding of place, and a sense of baroque delight to my calm interiors.

In 42 Old Church Street in Chelsea we have set the entire house around three different courtyard gardens, all beautifully designed by Tom Stuart-Smith so that each room flows into its garden and every walk and view terminates with green. Most importantly the windows of all the rooms can open onto gardens during temperate or hot times of the year, when the trees and planting deliver shade, cool and fresh air.

It is these sensations of views and of space flowing inwards and outwards, rather than the painstaking design of a building's parts that actually characterise my homes. But to achieve this effect, all elements must be carefully designed to play a self-effacing part, and surfaces must help to differentiate spaces and lead the eye from one place to another. This requires constant attention to detail and endless restraint. That is until it comes to the staircase design, which challenges the architect to create a totemic feature to give an individual identity to the whole house.

In the main, my homes aim to provide an elegant, characterful if discreet backdrop to people's lives. People should be encouraged to

*Opposite*
The window to the kitchen is focused to frame the seasonal changes of the woodlands.

*Overleaf*
A characterful staircase is always a welcome design challenge and gives personal character to a house. People have idiosyncratic tastes and sentimental attachments to their objects. I design simple interiors that can absorb their tastes.

stamp their personality on their homes through their choice of furniture and objects. The spaces need to be strong and clear enough to support people's activities, idiosyncratic tastes and choice of objects. I like objects for their aesthetics but also for their sentimental and emotional connotations. I anticipate that clients will want to exhibit their own objects, and I design that into their homes.

My small home is in a converted Victorian terrace set around a communal garden that, having survived the threat of total demolition and redevelopment in the 1960s, has matured and I now live facing an urban forest. The joys of living in such proximity to nature and in the heart of a city, 300m from shops and a tube station are inestimable – I count myself especially fortunate.

This form of dense urban housing arranged around substantial common gardens is one of the great treasures handed down by the late Victorians and remains a good starting point for high-density living in the future. Landscape is even more important in the city than it is in the countryside. Opening domestic spaces to balconies, gardens or greenery lends an enormous psychological boost and is another key element that enhances the pleasure or luxury of domestic life. In an age when we are looking for every opportunity to save energy and to enhance biodiversity, it is a 'no-brainer' that these types of substantial shared gardens provide free daylight, free cooling in summer, free year-round ventilation, free natural drainage and safe places for children to play. They also provide important habitat for urban flora and fauna.

New apartment buildings can be designed around new gardens. The buildings can be designed to be more flexible, more energy efficient, easier to maintain than their stucco fronted and slate-roofed Victorian counterparts. Most importantly, the tyranny of vertical division can be replaced by horizontal organisation that has fewer stairwells and greater flexibility to expand and contract.

This form of development projects strong streetscapes that invoke a sense of place, but the interior garden/courtyard as a shared focal point and safe amenity is the real social and environmental engine of community and quality of life.

Mass production is once again all the rage in house building, and so it should be. I say once again because almost 100 years ago the early Modernist movement extolled the virtues of prefabrication but associated it with the Modernist style of architecture. It is far more efficient to reduce time on site and far more effective to be

*Opposite*
Proximity to landscape in the city hugely increases well-being. High-density living arranged around communal gardens, a Victorian legacy, is a worthy starting point for new housing.

constructing building systems in the comfort of a dry, well-lit factory. But mass production need not necessitate a return to the dreary repetition synonymous with the 1960s. It can be decoupled from one architectural style or another. This means it can be deployed in the service of diverse architectures and can contribute to creating more varied townscapes.

A few years ago, we won an interesting ideas competition to replace Disneyland Paris' 1,000 log cabins located in an ancient wood a few kilometres from the main theme park. We collaborated with the engineer Karl Heinz who had roofed our Marylebone School in two days using a then-revolutionary four-inch-thick plywood called 'cross-laminated timber' or CLT.

Our brief was to develop a concept to deliver 1,000 fully-fitted, two-bedroom holiday homes for €60,000 each. The logistics of constructing 1,000 individual homes are mind-blowing. The idea of a thousand of anything in and around the same area is wholly dispiriting. We therefore approached the problem from the global to the detail. We developed a core design that could be customised in simple ways to differ in plan and organisation of windows. We developed a range of finishes that could be directly applied to the timber inner face of the CLT. We then developed alternative cladding systems for the outside of the structures using different materials, textures, colours and designs.

Computers were programmed to apply these individual settings to the production line and direct robots to laser-cut the different shapes without re-tooling. We calculated that four different houses would come off the production line per day. Each building fitted on a single truck, and a truck was despatched every six hours from Austria to France on a 24-hour journey to offload and return. On arrival in the forest, discrete corkscrew foundations would have been installed by the ground crews who were ready to receive the delivery, assemble the fully-fitted kit and connect to the network of environmental and energy services.

At the masterplan level we worked with Fulcrum engineers and landscape architect Jonnie Bell to make the servicing of those buildings in terms of energy, heat, water and waste and integrate them into the ecology of the forest — a tall order given the population density. We developed an encampment matrix made up of 30 independent hamlets that were laid out to create an instant sense of community for the transient residents. We placed car parks a short distance from

*Opposite*
Our buildings are the backdrop to other people's lives and are designed for them to use and adapt freely.

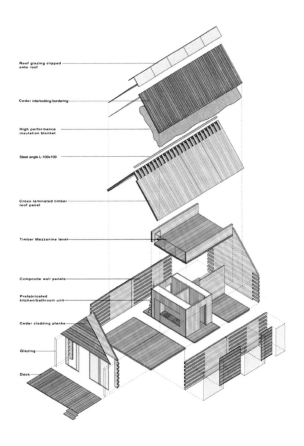

Roof glazing clipped
onto roof

Cedar interlocking bordering

High performance
insulation blanket

Steel angle L-100x100

Cross-laminated timber
roof panel

Timber Mezzanine level

Composite wall panels

Prefabricated
kitchen/bathroom unit

Cedar cladding planks

Glazing

Deck

the cabins. We made obvious walking trails from these hamlets that followed a series of small brooks leading visitors out of the woods to the reception area, from which electric transport to the theme park was provided.

The concept characterises a holistic design approach that considered place-making to manufacture, from the general to the detail. This design effort is in great excess of the quantum of design commissioned by volume house builders when they tackle the far more important task of building real permanent homes for our future communities.

Harnessing mass production is open to all forms of construction, from inner city tower buildings and apartment blocks to high-density suburban settlements. However, as the quantum of units increases, so the problem gets more complex and expands into place-making. Volume house builders rely on perfecting the mass fabrication of their units and cramming them onto sites with just enough road space for access. Rarely is proper thought given to generating a sense of community, conviviality, beauty, energy efficiency or environmental benefit. When I look at the dead hand of the 'volume' housing suppliers as their products attach themselves to every edge of every village, town and city, I rue the blatant lack of design input and the wealth of opportunities missed.

Occasional examples do spring up that are spearheaded by visionary local authorities or land owners. Mole Architects have recently delivered a community-driven, low-energy co-housing project in Cambridge with TOWN development; Peter Barber consistently delivers characterful inner city communities with local housing associations; Niall McLaughlin delivered a brilliant infill apartment building for Peabody; Stephen Taylor Architects have produced sensitive interventions of pocket housing, and there are many more excellent examples. All are working to strict financial constraints and all have produced award-winning, energy efficient buildings that are warmly embraced by the communities they serve. We need to encourage these trends and, crucially, adjust the planning and procurement systems to support all those developers and landowners that are seeking more inspiring long-term results.

A few years ago, we were invited to prepare housing proposals to replace a defunct recreation facility in suburban Cirencester. The existing building was set within mature trees with good access from a main road and surrounded by individual houses with medium-sized

*Opposite top*
Each unit is a variation of a basic design, fabricated off-site, delivered and assembled in 24-hours.

*Opposite bottom*
Buildings are arranged in groups of 30 to create individual hamlets.

gardens. We used this commission to explore a different type of higher-density suburban housing aimed at a diverse range of home-owners from families to the elderly and first-time buyers. The aim was to lay the foundations of a properly interwoven community of all ages within the existing mature woodland. We approached the project with a more urban mindset to see whether we could develop a more interesting, higher-quality, flexible scheme, a place with some individual identity and sense of community for the same overall development cost including land, infrastructure and landscaping of a conventional volume building project. The scheme took advantage of the slope of the site to cut and cover car parking, and this allowed us to introduce an open-air pedestrian space at the heart of the scheme where people might naturally congregate or at least use for everyday access. A range of housing typologies makes up the overall development and includes dedicated accommodation for the elderly. Each property has a small garden and an equal share of the large gardens and allotments that surround the development.

Back in London, we were commissioned to design a small apartment block in St John's Wood to replace a semi-detached house could make a small addition to the housing stock, with a building that could offer a range of tenancies, geared towards families, students, the elderly and start-ups. The proposed building is made of timber CLT components that are fast to erect. The building is on the edge of financial feasibility and will only happen if the developer spends a great deal on winning planning consent. The feasibility of the project is not helped by the requirement to provide free affordable housing which is likely to stymie the delivery of the additional 14 units. Ironically were the situation reversed and the council paid the developer to provide some affordable units within the scheme, the scheme would be financially viable. These types of relatively small increments of housing stock add up, but we have to apply great sensitivity when we try to insert projects into existing neighbourhoods.

My own family leads a reasonably private life, but the simple fact that we share a common 'walk' to our homes means that we see our 20 neighbours, know every one of them by name, can spot a rowdy Airbnb visitor, check that our elderly neighbour is not struggling home with an over-heavy shopping bag, send our kid to a neighbour's house when we are late coming home, get roped into the residents' association and know that we are all there for each other in an emergency. Even this level of 'community-lite' is critical and valuable. Well-

*Opposite top*
An experiment in mid-density suburban development. Existing open green spaces are preserved as shared gardens and allotments. Cars are parked *below* the development and a central pedestrian 'walk' forms a small shared communal place.

*Opposite bottom*
A new apartment on a pocket site in central London calibrating two scales of building. The new building adds 14 housing units to a site that previously had only two. These interval sites can be sensitively developed to deliver urgently needed mixed housing without upsetting the balance of our conservation areas.

considered design of layout, of visibility, of access and amenity is fundamental to generating good housing for even fairly private people like ourselves.

Even towers can be humanised and 'communitised', and once again architects have been addressing this across the globe. In our proposals for City Tower in central London, the base of the building was conceived as the social hub, with rooms that are rented out for events, with the all-important porter and spaces that connect into the public realm. The form of the building was broken into multiple sections that shared communal sky garden terraces. A glass wrapper insulates the building, and winter gardens ensure good natural ventilation and places for plants. Apartments overlook each other just enough to gain a sense of community but screened enough to protect privacy.

The scarcity of public housing is crippling the younger generation and leading private developers to provide ever more compacted accommodation. It is worth asking ourselves just how vulnerable we are to the appeal of rentable mass-produced micro-units that seamlessly stream our recorded decorative or viewing preferences onto our walls, and that no longer even require kitchens because meals are delivered to the door. With ever cheaper technology, algorithms can monitor and co-ordinate our choices in ever more attractive and invasive ways. Students would be the first target for this new market. Already our cities are littered with purpose-built student accommodation organised like glorified self-storage facilities comprising highly prototyped micro-units linked by faceless corridors. This dystopian, self-contained future is around the corner and is potentially challenging the social character of home life. Communal life is out of the cost equation. Or is it?

Thankfully from time to time society fights back, and the younger generations in particular are now counterattacking about climate change, healthier foods and wellbeing and all these trends and concerns are being picked up and responded to by mainstream commercial suppliers. I hope the same pressures will lead to the reintegration of community into housing projects and the encouragement of innovative pocket housing development in our inner cities and towns. If people continue to vote with their feet and if public housing projects can be properly curated, we can change our future for the better.

Working in Birmingham for Bennie Gray, an early commercial pioneer of urban renewal and the original mastermind behind the

*Opposite*
Towers can be humanised too. There are hundreds of examples worldwide of positive innovations in high-rise living. Here we introduce shared landscape terraces and break the whole into socially manageable communities.

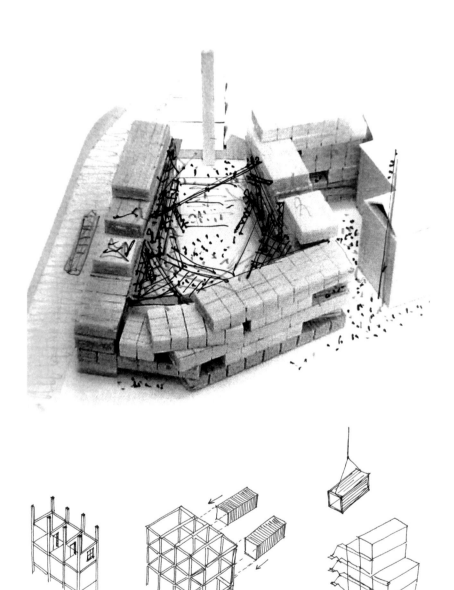

landmark Custard Factory renovation, we explored ways of extending his successful and quirky development onto an adjacent site that was earmarked for student accommodation. Bennie, who had dragged the Factory out of dereliction and into vibrant re-use, had proved that urban renewal was possible and provided the type of rich urban life that people sought.

The financial backbone of student housing is a simple cost-and-return calculation. Bottom line: it is profitable if you build cheap enough. Bennie looked to me to build cheap and yet keep the spirit of the place. We embraced the idea of off-site production and designed in flexible, lateral and vertical expansion to ensure a long-term use if demand for cellular student accommodation declined. The accommodation was arranged in linear blocks made up of prefabricated timber units. The block lined the canal and the main road, then turned inwards to form a new main entrance court to the old and new developments. The block wrapped itself around an internal courtyard that focused on the great preserved factory chimney. To the inside face we bolted a lattice work of public access ways, stairs and elevators, a type of vertical piazza made up of south-facing metal 'stoop' structures that we imagined would generate places for students to congregate and 'people watch', activities they crave but which modern life so readily relegates to social media.

There is a clear and present need in the UK to deliver housing on a massive scale. If only the country would deploy the nation's bountiful design talent to inspire innovative solutions for modern life.

*Opposite*
Mass off-site production of micro-units is upon us. The challenge is to use these minimalist living pods to create lively communities.

# EVERYTHING BUT THE BUILDING

Advocating change is a key pursuit
of architecture.

To be frank, it actually all started in 1978 in Paris after a small beer and an omelette in a café on the then run-down rue Saint-Denis. I was neither an architect nor studying to be one. I was an economist and art historian and I had ambitions to be a curator. I had come to Paris by coach to visit as many museums as I could. Inconceivable today, but in the 1970s it was perfectly possible to have heard about a new museum but not to have seen a single image of it, so I was heading to visit the new Museum of Modern Art and was excited by the prospect of its enormous 20th-century collection.

As I turned a final corner my eyes jumped out on stalks and I took a deep intake of breath. The Pompidou Centre was a building like no other. In a single moment I understood that it was architecture, above all the arts, that could most radically change the direction of society by modifying that most tangible embodiment of reality: the city. My strength of reaction was much due to my limited age and experience. To my young mind the city was only comprised of old and new conventional buildings and

seemed as fixed an unchangeable backdrop to everyday life as the establishment itself, both literally and metaphorically petrified and thereby unassailable. Here by contrast was the physical embodiment of new thinking, of a broader-minded society that was open to new forms of perception, new hierarchies and new hopes. Renzo Piano regularly refers to the building as 'young men's architecture'. For me it stands alone as the greatest single built expression of passionate youthful optimism and potential for change.

As I walked towards the building and into the swirling activity of the new piazza, I was set alight. Never before had I experienced a public space of such vitality, a space for fun, celebration, flirtation and conviviality, a place for the celebration of humanity rather than of pomp or national prestige. Pompidou launched society's trajectory towards a democratisation of its institutions, democratisation of its public spaces and all whilst shifting European architectural thinking away from the brutalist concrete architecture of the 1970s. Like Michelangelo centuries earlier at the Campidoglio Piazza,

Richard and Renzo succeeded in delivering more than the required building. They created a vibrant new public realm that connected into the pedestrian arteries of the city and up onto its façade and this owed a great deal to their experience and observations of the traditional Italian city.

Up until my damascene moment in Paris I had really only considered buildings as stand-alone objects, discrete entities like paintings or sculptures that could be judged for their own qualities alone. Up until that moment I had barely registered their importance as the literal building-blocks of streets or squares or for their magnetic influence on activity, pedestrian movement or social interaction.

Pompidou was a visionary project that just happened to be realised. Envisioning a 'better' future is a function embedded in our deeply uncynical and optimistic profession and much more so than in literature, painting, sculpture or film-making.

Envisaging change serves a critical part in nudging society towards new solutions. It is a type of advocacy that has been a characteristic of the architect's role in society since Vitruvius. Envisaging what can be done to modernise society, to combat poverty, to embellish the city, and then promoting those ideas as seductively as possible drives what we do. These are projects that in our heart of hearts we know will not happen even if we consciously delude ourselves into professing that they will. I consider this evidences the unrestrained optimism of our profession and a key purpose of our work.

*London as it could be*

*London as it could be, Royal Academy, London, UK:* The experience of the Pompidou Centre both as a beacon of change and in its encouragement of participatory street-life enthralled my younger self and led me a few years later to bluff my way into an apprenticeship at the Richard Rogers Partnership, a relationship that lasted for two decades and involved collaborating with Richard on developing and advocating his ideas and philosophy. What is so fascinating to recognise, in hindsight, is that his constant advocacy of public space and our many unrealised projects have been as influential as the built work.

In 1986 Richard was invited to participate in a major architecture exhibition at the Royal Academy: 'Fosters Rogers Stirling'. The three architects were at the forefront of world architecture and the RA had decided that this was the moment to celebrate their work by putting the entire gallery at their disposal. Richard chose the largest room and elected to use the entire exhibition budget to design a public realm project for central London with the idea that we would simply pin the drawings up on the walls. Laurie Abbott spearheaded the project with his clear thinking, incredible drawings and wonderful sculptural skills. I worked with Laurie, co-ordinated the project and with John Andrews designed the exhibition as an imposing installation piece replete with a 15m-long reflective pool in the main gallery, despite the RA's withering protestations. On the opening night, the irrepressible James Stirling secretly launched a pair of beautiful goldfish into our pool and the evening was complete.

Between us we conceived and illustrated a powerful and seductive argument for improving the public realm of central London from Trafalgar Square to Waterloo station and from the Houses of Parliament to Blackfriars. The proposals argued for the benefits of investing in the then very neglected public realm. The exhibition championed pedestrianisation, public space, walking and cycling at a time when these were far from mainstream concerns. The result, direct or indirect, 30 years later can be seen in the many projects by others, including the pedestrianisation of Trafalgar Square, the new bridges strapped to the sides of Charing Cross Bridge and the plethora of interventions aimed at improving the experience of the city: all examples of pure advocacy reaping great rewards for the city.

*Previous*
Competition drawing for the Piano + Rogers Centre Georges Pompidou.

*Opposite*
Trafalgar Square 'as it could be' 1986 without cars and buses. The Square was subsequently pedestrianised in 2003.

*Overleaf*
The exhibition installation at the Royal Academy replete with 15m reflecting pool crossed by the proposed new bridge at Charing Cross. The irrepressible architect James Stirling famously launched a pair of beautiful goldfish into the pool on the opening night.

*London as it could be*

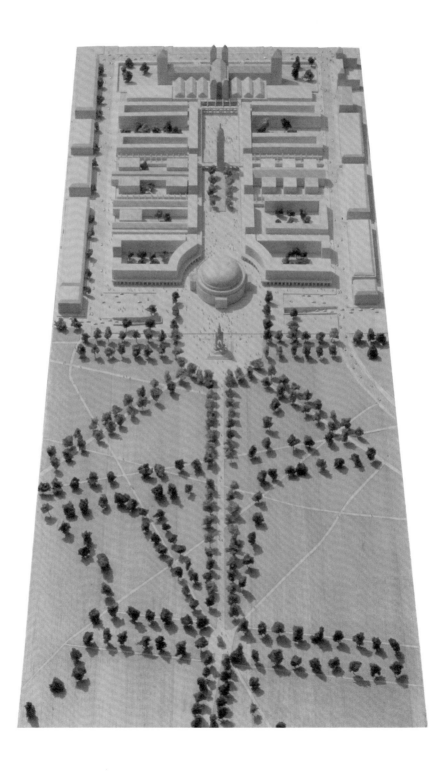

*Albertopolis 2025, Kensington, London, UK:* Albertopolis stretches from the Albert Memorial to the Natural History Museum on Cromwell Road. The campus had been purchased with the profits of the Great Exhibition of 1851. Originally used as the showground for agricultural and other exhibitions, the site was incrementally filled in with educational buildings, museums and their endless extensions.

In 1988, when I was completing my architectural studies on the site at the Royal College of Art, I was dismayed to find that despite attracting over three million visitors a year and having a standing student population of many thousands, Albertopolis showed no visible signs of public life, no shops and no restaurants or cafés. Far from being an animated metropolitan cultural district as might have been expected, the public realm was a desert bereft of all signs of life besides the coaches collecting or discharging visitors. Prince Albert's vision of 'Place' had been abandoned in favour of an ever-greater ramble of institutional buildings.

My proposal, Albertopolis 2025, was to set out how a vibrant metropolitan public realm could be integrated at the heart of this historic district. Using the geometry of the 19th-century axis set out by Albert himself, the proposal ran from the centre of the Royal Kensington Gardens to the National History Museum on Cromwell Road in the South. I proposed to re-route Kensington Road into a tunnel in order to create a seamless sequence of pedestrianised spaces from the park around the Albert Memorial and Hall across a shared university campus green to the foot of the restored Imperial College tower. From there, a south-facing grand stairway through a colonnaded screen led into a new Museums' Square onto which each museum faced, and onto which the Natural History Museum had originally been designed to address with its monumental towers. These inner public spaces were accessible by pedestrians coming from Exhibition Road and Queen's Gate through covered shopping gallerias, themselves lined in arcades for retail, cafés and bookshops.

I can't say what influence, if any, the project has had. At the time, the 1851 Commissioners showed little interest, but the tireless Peter Murray included it in his 'Contemporary Architects' show at the Royal Academy and then travelled the show internationally. That promotion may have generated the grit in the oyster that drew attention to the greater opportunities of the campus and instigated the many initiatives and improvements that have taken place since those days.

*Opposite*
Albertopolis 2025 envisaged a public realm initiative – a sequence of active public spaces at the heart of the cultural district established by Prince Albert with the proceeds from the 1851 Exhibition. The proposed scheme restored the original axis and created a series of connected public spaces that ran from the Natural History Museum in the south to the centre of Kensington Gardens in the north.

*Cities for a small planet, Faber & Faber:* In 1995 Richard Rogers was the first architect to be invited to deliver the BBC Reith Lectures and I was fortunate to help him write it. Our main ambition was to promote the idea of the city as being at the heart of the environmental and social crisis and therefore at the heart of its resolution. Specifically, we argued that an increasing majority of people would live in cities causing the majority of consumption and thus pollution. We advocated the application of 'precautionary principle' to safeguard our species' future on the planet.

We assembled the environmental arguments from the likes of Herbert Girardet and the social ones from the likes of Mike Davis and Jane Jacobs. We used Richard's work to describe tangible solutions to some of those environmental and social issues and showcased the pioneering work of city mayors including Jaime Lerner in Curitiba, Brazil, and Pascal Maragal in Barcelona, Spain.

The lectures and their later publication in book form as *Cities for a small planet* aimed to be a wake-up call and led to Richard being invited to head the government's Urban Task Force, which was the UK's most high-profile attempt to map out how the design of the built environment could set a clear path towards a sustainable environmental and social future.

*Opposite*
Published in no fewer than seven languages, *Cities for a small planet* highlighted the environmental and social consequences of the ever-increasing expansion of cities. The book proposed an approach to tackling the problems of our growing cities and heralded Richard Rogers's chairmanship of the UK government's Urban Task Force focused on sustainable development.

_Giant Recycled Paper Building, Millennium Dome, London, UK:_ When I finally left the Richard Rogers Partnership in 1998, Ben Evans, friend and fellow collaborator on Mark Fisher's and Richard Rogers's book _A New London_, persuaded me to help out on the Millennium Exhibition and in particular on the Community Zone, the original design for which had failed to gain the support of the star chamber of millennium grandees.

There were twelve 'zones' housed in the Millennium Exhibition under the massive lightweight roof of the Millennium Dome, (now the O2 centre) an incredible structure that its architect, Mike Davies, Rogers's partner, boasted was lighter than the air contained within it. Creating a 'pavilion' that would in some way resonate with, touch or involve the diverse communities around the UK seemed a tall order, especially given the political motivation to be accessible and ensure politically correct interpretations of inclusiveness.

Ever the optimist, I launched into an approach that explored people and community in the context of their counterpart private and public spaces. The exhibition was to be a 20-minute 'experience' divided into three sections that explored the individual and the room; the neighbour and the street; and the citizen and the city. The sub-themes were of social integration and environmental sustainability. I took the view not to depict society's diversity but instead to focus on its common humanity, as people divided into generational cycles as catalogued in the 'seven ages of man'. My purpose was to expose generational characteristics in the hope that that might induce some common understanding and empathy across all generations.

Working on the Millennium Project was like being a kid in a sweetshop because the whole creative community of the UK were, although a little cynical about the exhibition, persuadable that they should play their part in contributing to make it a powerful cultural moment in our history. I could pick up the phone to literally anyone and know that they would at least grant me a chance to pitch for their involvement.

Seven 3m×3m cubes were arranged by artist Robert Wilson, with each 'age' interpreted by seven contemporary artists, from Mark Wallinger to Sarah Raphael, Webster and Noble to Eduardo Paolozzi, known and unknown living treasures. These cohorts were then led through the 'street' where the Cardboard Citizens theatre company disguised as members of the public initiated happenings that drew strangers together through shared laughter or surprise.

_Opposite_
This working cardboard model illustrates the spectacular form of the pavilion, with its columns specially made from paper recycled from cardboard swatches donated by the children of Britain. The structural columns range from 10m to 20m at its apex.

The last room was a giant abstracted model of the idealised 'sustainable' city of the future, described in a series of films 'sampled' from all over the country by recent British Film School graduates. This material was streamed into multiple contemporaneous projections that described the 24-hour cycle of the sustainable city in six minutes. Each individual film was projected within the model buildings, and not one figure was ever more than 6 inches tall — a veritable Lilliputian city that I hoped would leave young children with the life-long memory of having visited Lilliput for real, and hopefully with the take-out message of the importance of community and environmental sustainability.

The exhibition was housed in a pavilion that I argued should be made entirely from recycled material donated by the children of Britain. All British children since the 1960s were brought up on a diet of initiatives launched periodically by the BBC's *Blue Peter* programme. For generations these initiatives have drawn in parents and grandparents supporting their offspring's projects for charity. My sisters and I, for example, had with our mother's help collected bags full of aluminium milk-bottle tops that were then sent to the BBC, made into ingots and sold for the benefit of children in Biafra. The national status of the project meant we were able to enlist the help of the BBC. The *Blue Peter* programme officially unveiled the pavilion to 1.5 million young viewers and launched the campaign.

The logistics of collecting material from as far away as the Outer Hebrides was formidable and I had alighted on using paper in open reference to Shigeru Ban's work on small-scale paper buildings. We requested children to send in five pieces of waste cardboard (cereal packs, etc) cut to the size of a CD cover with the name of the recycling paper mill on one side and their own name on the other. These little packages were light enough to be sent by second-class post from anywhere in the country, and I considered this entirely affordable and therefore easily and equitably assessible to all. Once announced, the race was on because the first 25,000 donors were to become the official benefactors and have their names affixed to the building.

I enlisted friend and colleague Stephen Spence to collaborate on the design and the advice of Shigeru Ban on how to procure and fireproof a paper building of this magnitude. We designed a bespoke set of architectural construction components for the structure, walls, and cladding of the building, all fabricated from recycled paper. Our aim was to create a visceral connection between children and the possibilities of design and engineering, to show that there were no

*Opposite*
The Cardboard Street during assembly, showing the complete hierarchy of fireproof cardboard architectural elements specifically designed for the project. The names of the first 25,000 children to send in their cardboard donations were affixed to the building as its benefactors.

limits to the power of participation and to the imagination's ability to transform even humble recycled materials cut out of the back of cereal packets.

At the end of the Millennial year the spectacular building was demolished, pulped and reused as the material for a book that documented the making of the building, replete with a small cardboard kit from which the children could make their own recycled building as a souvenir.

The overall Millennium Experience was rounded on as being the hubris of Tony Blair's government, but days before the opening, while the jury was still out, esteemed architectural critic Marcus Binney visited the Dome and described our design thus: 'Topping them all for sheer beauty is Shared Ground — an extraordinary cardboard structure'. This was most welcome, since it was also the last UK review the building received.

*Opposite top*
View of the soaring 20m-high 'wing' shortly after its erection under the Millennium Dome.

*Opposite bottom*
At the end of the year 2000 celebrations, the cardboard building was dismantled and re-pulped and the paper used for a memorial book that included a cardboard model kit of the building.

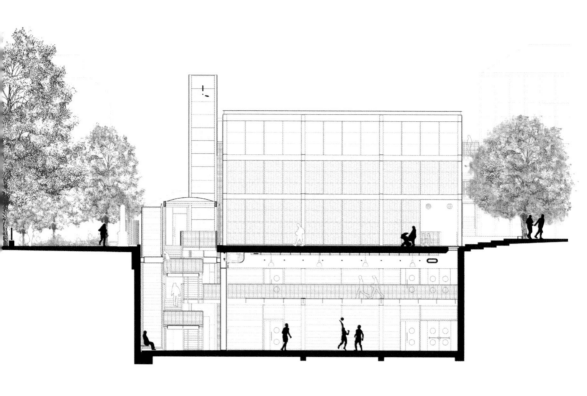

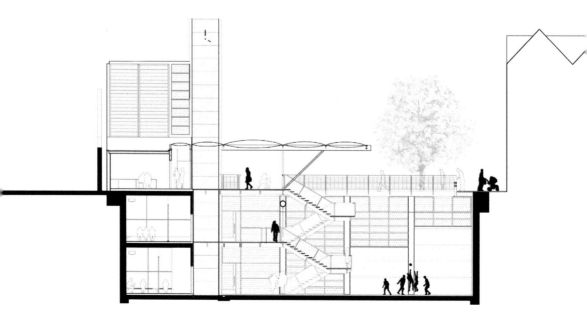

St Marylebone School, Westminster, London, UK: I was invited to help the formidable Elizabeth Phillips OBE, the then head of St Marylebone School in central London. This record-busting state school had 900 girls, a tiny site in a conservation area, a protected mature tree, only five per cent of the recommended quota of open space, and no money.

Elizabeth optimistically explained that, as a newly promoted Performing Arts School, they needed to add a gymnasium, dance studios, music and art departments. The consequences of not delivering the plan was they would have to up sticks and move out of the inner city. The situation posed an existential threat to the continuation of the school at the heart of its urban community. Elizabeth's proposed solution was to cut down the tree, build the facility on the car park (up to and in front of a listed building) and sacrifice whatever was left of the five per cent open space. She was eager to hear my thoughts.

I had resisted ordering wine during our lunch, and this helped me refrain from giving an instant assessment of the feasibility of her approach in planning terms alone. I went away a little dejected by yet another dead-end commission. I had been taught by the great architect James Gowan that the brain should be left alone to work things out. Often one wakes up with a brilliant idea and considers that a good night's sleep had done the job, but as James explained, nothing of the sort: while we sleep the brain is busy trying to make sense of the seemingly unresolvable.

It took a few good nights' sleep until the solution emerged: bury the gymnasium, ditch the car park and create a new playground on top of it. Two problems solved. Elizabeth loved the idea. I carried out a desktop study of the site only to discover that the car park sat over a defunct cemetery that spanned from the medieval period until the early 19th century. Permanent residents included artist George Stubbs, sculptor John Michael Rysbrack, bare-knuckle boxing champion George Figgs and the Wesley family tomb (excepting John the Methodist founder who was buried elsewhere), and none had immediate plans to leave. My brain had clearly been asleep at the helm and had not counted on this possibility.

There is no better example of the critical role played by a client body than at St Marylebone: a formidable head, a powerhouse of a board of governors and lateral-thinking Diocesan Director of Building (it is a Church of England school) Steve White who, when

Opposite top
Drawing showing how the large gymnasium was introduced into the small site with a new Astroturfed playground/teaching area established above.

Opposite bottom
The new lift gave accessibility for the first time to the whole school by connecting to previously wheelchair inaccessible floors..

confronted with my unaffordable proposition, sent me on my way with the sphinx-like instruction to 'spend more money and solve more problems'.

My response was to propose demolishing a perfectly good, small art building and by doing so incorporate two extra floors of dance studios under it and a new three-storey arts and music block above. The project gained efficiencies and delivered better value for money. Critically, decoupling the building from the existing art block made the whole development exempt from tax, a further financial boost. Five problems solved. Architecture is an incredible human endeavour, a true creative collaboration between many minds from inception through to construction. Architects are merely the tip of a very big pencil.

Having established the concept for the design, I challenged myself to deliver a large, below-ground facility that would nonetheless enjoy the qualities of fresh air and light associated with being above ground. Normally an underground facility requires air-conditioning, artificial light and multiple space-guzzling escape routes. A couple of key observations of historic buildings had convinced me that this apparent contradiction could be overcome. The first was the experience of the great quality of light gained within a small courtyard connected to the massive flank of Westminster Abbey. The second was a visit to a restored mercantile home in Shiraz that had a substantial basement to which the occupants decanted during the blazing hot summer months.

The underground gymnasium was thus linked to an open courtyard. Its orientation meant that sunlight penetrates deep into the space in early morning, and as the sun moves round so light is reflected into the space off the light-coloured concrete walls. The gymnasium is cooled in the summer and heated in the winter by the constant temperature of the ground that naturally radiates through the concrete retaining walls that have, contrary to regulations, been left uninsulated. In practice, heating is fitted but hardly ever required and ventilation is entirely provided by retractable single-glazed 'fire station' doors that allow the space of the gymnasium to flow directly into the courtyard during the temperate months. The courtyard becomes the 'free' environmental engine of the development. The budget conventionally spent on enclosing and ventilating a fire escape was used to turn the open-air stair into a dramatic sculptural element as seen from both inside and outside.

*Opposite*
The building is five storeys tall from gymnasium to art department. The stair provides fun and a sculptural drama that is greatly enhanced by the theatre of movement at break times.

*Overleaf*
The large below-ground open courtyard is the environmental engine of the project. It collects sun and daylight and provides fresh air free to the Gymnasium. Sunlight and daylight bounce off the concrete walls. The large façade has retractable glazed fire station doors. The basement is cooled in the summer and warmed in the winter by the constant temperature of the ground.

Above, we sought an appropriate architectural treatment to bed the new building into its setting. We used red Corten steel to echo the colour of the listed buildings opposite and across the street. The lift shaft was extended to read like a church bell-tower over the commemorative gardens and as a school clock tower over the playground.

In architectural detail terms, we strove to use the state school budget to create what looks like tailored detailing. In fact, we moulded the waterproof concrete structural walls to look like bespoke architectural elements, used standard industrial electrical cable trays as ceilings and handrails, used silk duvets for acoustic ceilings, felt on walls and other commonly available industrial materials.

The ultimate achievement of the project was to turn every problem on its head and to deliver value where it was least expected. The new network of open spaces transformed the internal organisation of the school and then seamlessly integrated the whole campus into an improved overall urban context. New views towards neighbouring heritage buildings were generated to subtly colour the everyday experience of the new campus. None of which was a requirement of the brief, but all were as a consequence of a collaborative design-led approach that sought out opportunities wherever they could be found.

The building received many awards and accolades and I mention this because we should, as a matter of course, expect our public projects to produce exceptional results. The project would not have been possible had it not been for the flexibility and inventiveness of the client body. Had it been evaluated by the standardised project management tools required under most public procurement regimes, the project would never have got off the ground.

If we, through our governments and in this time of crisis, are to enjoy the full benefits of creative thinking, then our public administration needs to be up to the task of supporting innovative lateral thinking. The increasing attractiveness of inflexible financial assessments makes society vulnerable to missing a host of useful benefits that our human imagination can generate. In a period of our history when we are challenged by social and environmental problems, cutting off the lifeline of innovative thinking would be a great administrative failing.

*Opposite*
The lift tower acts as a school clock tower over the playground. The Astroturf surface of the new playground is soft to the touch and has become a favoured meeting-place as well as a sports teaching area.

*Overleaf*
The clock stands like a church tower over the commemorative gardens linking the school to the street. The gardens were designed by Todd Longstaffe-Gowan. The red Corten cladding of the Arts and Music building echoes the rich colouring of the 19th-century redbrick buildings opposite.

St Marylebone School

*Youth Club, Stowmarket*

_Youth Club, Stowmarket, UK:_ Following the success of the School, we were invited in 2009 by the visionary Sorrell Foundation to design one of the Blair government's 30 new nationwide youth clubs. The government had resolved to address juvenile crime and alienation by initiating a programme of youth clubs aimed at getting kids off the street and into an environment where positive pursuits could be encouraged and supported. The visionary John and Frances Sorrell had challenged the government to commission innovative architects to dream up these new places and the government had promptly reverted by handing the whole project over to their Foundation.

For the past 40 or so years in the UK we have seen a shift in society's respect for and attitude to public buildings. Long ago the term 'civic' was universally adopted to describe a style of architecture that was proud and formal, if somewhat patronising. These buildings often came across as the state granting favours to a grateful populace. They were stately and patriotic but certainly not sympathetic or inclusive. Efforts were made to soften this image and to create buildings of a more inclusive character, but frankly they tended to dumb down to an unfairly perceived 'level' of the users. The process also went hand in hand with a revolution in public procurement that aimed at reducing the cost of construction but simply resulted in the previous high standards of design and construction being reduced to a mixed bag of 'cheap and cheerful' hybrid styles, fitted out like basic office buildings — except, that is, on the rare occasions that quality of architecture has been sought out and implemented.

The Sorrells were aiming high. These youth centres were to be beacons of hope and change. For starters, the clients were to be the children themselves. They were to be entrusted with guiding the project from its inception, including briefing the architect. I travelled up to Stowmarket not sure what to expect from the client body that I had been told was made up of young people who were mostly in some form of trouble or care, either because of drugs, arson, truancy or because they had learning difficulties or had been abused.

We met in a beautiful old council room. Fifteen or so young people were assembled around a large table, their minders and social workers seated behind them. They sat patiently as I presented my past work. Once finished, I opened the discussion to the floor. What is life like in Stowmarket for the younger generation; what kind of place do you want; what facilities would be useful; what would attract other children to this place?

_Opposite_
The Sorrell Foundation insisted that the young were the clients and would direct the design development of their building.

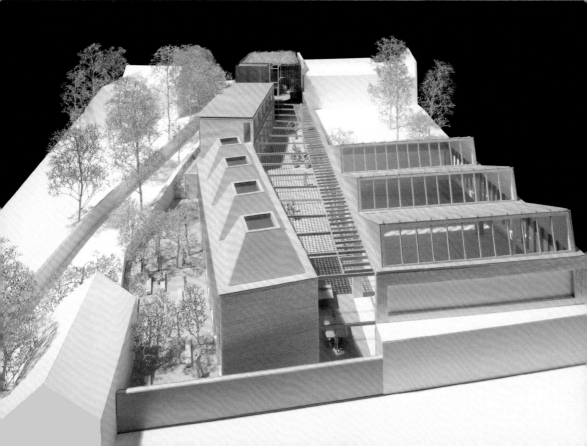

The group of teenagers had never met each other before and a total silence unsurprisingly ensued. But eventually and after a little coaxing from the Sorrell co-ordinator Jen Olsen, one boy plucked up all his courage to break the ice: 'I think we should have place where we could have tea and biscuits'. This small step received the immediate approval of the group who nodded in unanimous confirmation. An unremarkable start for this £3 million project, but the prelude to an amazing journey of rapid learning and development in which these young people flourished and flowered in front of my eyes. If ever I needed convincing of the universal power of education to inspire, then this experience did it. It transpired that not one member of the group had visited a museum nor had even travelled to London. In three short months, Jen was to expand their cultural horizons with trips to the capital, workshops with the Pentagram graphic design studio and much, much more. The more that was thrown at them, the more they absorbed and processed, and the more they felt empowered and were communicative.

This said it took all Jen's powers of persuasion to divert the group from calling their club the 'Stowmarket Independents Club' or SIC for short. They eventually alighted on 'The Mix' for their home-from-home, or in some cases their home from no home at all. The Mix contained a range of facilities, from a street-level Hopper-esque diner run by apprentice chefs, a hall above where meetings, talks and readings would take place (one of the group was a secret writer), recording studios, carpentry workshops and a gymnasium, all huddled around a large internalised two-storey public covered space replete with graffitied walls, table tennis, beanbags and a fireplace around which people could drop in to chat and see what was going on. The public space flowed in from the street and into a lower level where the social support services (counselling, sex education, advice) were discreetly accessible without fuss.

The process concluded with the group presenting their scheme to the Suffolk committee that was represented by the Mayor, the Chief of Constabulary, Social Services and more dignitaries. The presentation was rehearsed and choreographed by the students and lasted twenty minutes. They were effervescent with excitement and pride. It was followed by a question-and-answer session where the mother of one of my clients approached me with tears in her eyes to tell me that she had never seen her son stand up for anything in his entire life but there he was, and she pointed to the boy bent over

*Opposite top*
The Youth Club's new Assembly Hall sits boldly on the High Street. The entrance to the club is alongside a glazed 'Hopper-esque' diner run by the young and leads into the covered street that is their main meeting-place.

*Opposite bottom*
Each building echoes the local industrial history of Stowmarket with factory or oast-house-type roof silhouettes.

*Youth Club, Stowmarket*

the model passionately and politely defending the scheme to a local resident, who predictably found the style of architecture far too modern for Stowmarket.

Public buildings, education and inclusiveness are powerful tools that society needs to grab with both hands and use to empower and innovate. The UK is still half-hearted about it. The Mix was completed in 2017 with young people's involvement. However, the Local Authority eschewed our involvement and appointed a design & build contractor to reinterpret our design. Rather than the rich spatial sequences and the industrial chic we had successfully delivered at Marylebone, they edited out the public spaces and used bland internal finishes, all in the name of managed, cost-effective procurement protocols.

The addition of beauty, drama or interest to our lives in the public realm and in our public buildings rests entirely in the hands of those who manage procurement.

*Opposite*
The Youth Club was characterised by its covered meeting-place where the young could gather at the heart of the building before using the dedicated facilities.

*Tate Tower, Bankside*

Tate Tower, Bankside, London, UK: Occasionally a public project of magnitude comes along to spearhead regeneration. The Tate Modern was publicly funded to occupy the Bankside Power Station and instigate the regeneration of the large post-industrial area on the south of the River Thames at the heart of London facing St Paul's Cathedral. The redevelopment of a small site next to the Tate marked our attempt to combine private and public enterprise to launch high-quality change.

In 1999 when the practice was in its infancy, architect Kevin Dash had generously invited me to share his very smart office in Covent Garden. Kevin was previously design director of a large commercial practice but had forgone the trappings of a large office and reverted to his main passion, getting back to hands-on design of exquisite buildings that included the headquarters of the Bank Audi in Beirut. Kevin had been selected to redevelop a small paper depository building on Hopton Street, literally on doorstep of the new Tate.

I watched from a few desks away as a medium-sized elegant building emerged on his drawing-board until I could resist no longer. I suggested that given that the Tate was not listed, that our building sat within a run-down regeneration zone, and that the Tate had been publicly funded to spearhead regeneration, he should perhaps push the boat out and propose a scheme that matched the artistic ambition and regeneration purpose of the Tate Modern itself.

Kevin, who wisely prefers not putting his head above the parapet, eventually fell under my spell and let me indulge in the fantasy of proposing a glass beacon that matched the height and width of the chimney of the Tate Modern, and that signalled the start to the Tate's magnificent ramped entrance. To offset this extraordinary incursion into the London skyline we proposed what we considered to be 'public benefits': to reshape the base of our building to improve the sequence of arrival to the ramped entrance of the Tate, to include activities at the lower levels that would energise or activate the public space that separated the site from the monolithic Tate, and to produce a building of exceptional sculptural slenderness and quality of build.

With the support of the brilliant then Director of Planning at Southwark, Fred Manson, we shaved a third of the site off for public street improvements and included restaurants and cafés on the first two floors. These were designed to spill out and activate the relatively dead space around the monolithic building. Fred had set out his observation that large institutional buildings tended to 'freeze'

*Opposite*
First collage sketch illustrating the proposal to create a glass tower that echoed the proportions and height of the Tate Modern's emblematic chimney stack.

*Overleaf*
The Tower signals the dramatic ramped side entrance to the Tate Modern's massive Turbine Hall. We had hoped that our building would herald a series of slim point towers that would surround and crown the great solid mass of the Tate Modern.

the areas around them. He saw our building that was located within an intimate distance from the side of the massive Tate as having the potential to develop an active space that could generate life outside the bulwark of the Tate.

The project was immensely political and was reviewed by the then Mayor of London Ken Livingstone at a GLA design review. The Mayor had recently initiated the current policy that each private development should provide at its own expense an equal amount of private and social housing units. The Mayor, who had no qualms about tall buildings especially when they were neither next to a listed building nor in a conservation area, saw our Tower as a potential flagship of this policy and welcomed the six storeys of affordable housing that made up the base of the Tower beneath the less affordable 16 apartments above. A 20-storey variation of the design gained planning permission but was never built.

Building tall is an expensive proposition. Building tall and slim poses real engineering challenges. Selling large, expensive apartments on a regeneration site on the South Bank in the early 2000s meant that only quality could offset the perceived negatives of the location. But all these factors contrived to create a virtuous spiral of justifications for a highly crafted and ingeniously structured building by Chris Wise of Expedition Engineering. Moreover, we sought to revisit the notion of high-rise living that included introducing winter gardens to help insulation, south-facing terraces, and by working with Fulcrum Engineering we developed the building's services to increase energy efficiency by among other things using the structure to play its part in regulating the temperature of the building and reduce the need for cooling.

In purely financial terms, the repetitive nature of the structure meant that economies of scale rendered our highly tailored detailing affordable, and this played to our design strengths. Achieving an extremely high build quality for a residential building was an approach that until then was reserved for the office buildings sector.

But it was the manipulation of the spaces leading up to and around the base of the building that fascinated me the most and that drove my ambition to see the building built. The analysis of Volker Buttgereit of BMC fluid dynamics showed that the orientation of the building into the prevailing winds meant that this tall, thin structure had a minimal wind impact, but we curved the ends of the building to limit potential wind turbulence further. As visitors approached, they

*Opposite left*
The lifts and stairs are located to the west of the building, creating shade from the setting sun. Outriggers are strapped to the accommodation to compensate for the extreme slenderness of its form. A column of west-facing terraces shades the living rooms with their spectacular views of St Paul's and the City of London

*Opposite right*
Fireproof timber louvres shade the winter gardens and south-facing landscaped terraces creating stable environmental conditions inside. The north façade faces the spectacular view towards St Paul's Cathedral and is uninterrupted glass. The building's concrete structure is exposed internally and cooled by the constant temperature of local groundwater.

*Tate Tower, Bankside*

were eased around curved sides of the building and views opened up in a calibrated and dramatic manner. Seen from the square, the tall, curved shaft of our tower framed and emphasised the verticality of the great chimney of the Tate, and to my mind created a more visually and spatially interesting urban sequence of arrival to this major international destination.

A lower version of the tower gained planning permission at appeal, but politics and the recent construction of the Herzog & de Meuron ziggurat meant that deals were made that saw the development rights shifted to allow better views of the Tate's extension. We had hoped the tower might instigate a group of similar buildings and, eventually, a skyline of slender point towers around the great solid mass that is the Tate Modern, heralding a thoroughly new metropolitan district of London, rising like a phoenix from its industrial past.

*Opposite*
Setting the new building back
from its site boundaries
and curving its ends create
a more considered pedestrian
approach to the Tate Modern
and frame a dramatic view
of the Tate's chimney.

*Market Place, Wadhurst*

*Market Place, Wadhurst, East Sussex, UK:* I was fascinated by an invitation from Anthony Dunnett, the retired head of English Partnerships, the government's development arm, with whom I had worked on the Greenwich Peninsula Masterplan, the legacy of the Millennium Experience. He lived in the market town of Wadhurst in East Sussex, and was a trustee of the charity that owned the WW1 Memorial Hall. He and his fellow trustees were contemplating replacing the Hall with a building that could be better subdivided to generate more revenue.

Our starting point was to interrogate the workings of the whole town to reveal its centre of gravity and to test whether redevelopment could in some way benefit the life of the greater whole. Like so many towns, Wadhurst concentrated its activities along a high street that petered off at either end. The demolition of the Hall gave access to a large site at the centre of the high street that dropped down to a cricket pitch beyond that the charity also owned. Its removal opened views of the spectacular rolling Weald.

We proposed a secondary axis that led from the St Peter and St Paul Church in the north to the cricket pitch in the south. This was entirely pedestrianised save for the short hop across the high street. The site of the Memorial Hall was left open as a small square where moveable stalls could be deployed on market day. The steep change in level was bridged over to accommodate a lower-level medical suite that was lit from a side garden and reachable by car from a lower-level access road. Three new retail buildings lined the square and led to a new stepped Memorial garden that acted as amphitheatre for the cricket pitch where large events took place throughout the year.

The replacement cultural centre edged the new Memorial gardens and was flanked by new tennis courts that decked over the large car park. A new restaurant was perched over the cricket pitch and enjoyed long views over the Weald. We anticipated weddings and events starting at the church and making their way along the new pedestrian route with receptions held at the new restaurant.

The replacement of a single strategically located building gave the town a new centre for public life at the heart of its high street.

*Opposite*
Replacing the Memorial Hall on a new site opened up a crucial space at the heart of the high street for a new Market Place and public Memorial Gardens, bringing a new axis of activity to the town.

*Centre Pompidou-Metz, France:* Collaboration is a wonderful process,

*Centre Pompidou-Metz, France:* Collaboration is a wonderful process, especially with people who have complementary skills. Shigeru Ban is now an internationally renowned architect, the 2014 Pritzker Prize winner. In 1995 I had included his fascinating work in *Cities for a small planet* and we had become friends. After a couple of minor collaborations in 2003 he invited me to collaborate on the competition to design a satellite to the Centre Georges Pompidou in Paris on a massive empty regeneration site in the eastern French city of Metz, home to the great St Stephen Cathedral. The centre of operations was my new office studio that was soon filled with interns from around the world.

Counter-intuitively the awesome calibre of the competing architects meant there was less pressure on us to win. So we considered ourselves free to do what we thought best and frankly speaking we were quite taken aback when we actually won the competition.

Uppermost in my mind was how to integrate the building into its vast, flat, empty territory that to boot was on the wrong side of the railway tracks. We brought in Michel Desvigne to develop landscape ideas that could begin to characterise this empty, characterless place.

Unlike most museums with unassailable outer walls such as the Tate Modern, the Centre envisaged by Shigeru was a permeable place that harboured its masterpieces in inner buildings that were air-conditioned to museum standard. Together Michel and I developed the idea that the Centre expanded over the whole territory, like a giant octopus with invisible tentacles that spread out and drew people and activities to its heart. The proposed Jardin des Arts was therefore an integral part of the building and its artistic programme. It continued the democratising spirit of the original Centre Pompidou that drew people from the popular urban piazza into and up the façade of the building to the very doors of the galleries themselves.

The Jardin des Arts was a soft version of the urban Place Beaubourg in Paris and was edged by shallow, linear reflecting pools. These were frozen in winter to provide open-air ice rinks and were lined with cafés and shops. The main esplanade funnelled people onto a ramped entrance hall set under the tented roof that exaggerated the soaring forms of the gallery 'tubes' suspended above.

We likened the environmental concept of the Centre to an interpretation of a traditional Japanese house, with a large overhanging roof, paper-thin walls and a central hearth. The public spaces under the roof were conceived as tempered rather than conditioned spaces,

*Opposite*
The soaring timber roof of the centre encloses the spectacular public halls while the galleries and exhibits are cocooned within air-conditioned flexible galleries. The large enclosed volumes under the roof use the exhaust air from the galleries that is cooler than outside air in summer and warmer than outside air in winter, a basic energy reuse system.

*Overleaf*
Night-time transforms the building and reveals its spectacular skeletal structure and undulating forms.

Centre Pompidou-Metz

*Centre Pompidou-Metz*

heated in the winter using the exhaust heat from the inner galleries and cooled in the summer from the relatively cool exhaust from the same. The walls of the Centre could be opened in summer and closed down in winter. The roof, with its large eaves, provided shade in summer and protection from wind and rain in winter.

With the help of the amazing Swiss timber engineer Hermann Blummer, Shigeru pulled off the most extraordinary and spectacular feat of engineering in the form of a 100-m clear span 'sky' of sustainable timber grid-shell that magically comes to rest in swirling timber columns. The structure dazzles and amazes.

The Galleries themselves by contrast were highly disciplined, flexible, fully air-conditioned, efficiently organised spaces designed to the Pompidou's strict dimensional and functional brief for the constant turnover of 'permanent' exhibitions from the main collection. To complete the psychological integration of this 'outer city' building with the inner city, we pointed each Gallery towards a key city landmark with spectacular effect. The long tube-like rooms with their glazed gabled ends create a telescopic visual trick that greatly enlarges the apparent presence of landmarks such as the Gothic Cathedral and brings them into the Galleries as if they are exhibits. This dramatic visual effect completed the fusion of the building into its context.

*Opposite top*
The long flexible galleries create a telescopic visual effect that draws the iconic symbols of Metz deep into the galleries. This completes the integration of the building into the cultural life of the city.

*Opposite bottom*
The Gallery tubes pierce through the Centre's undulating roof.

*Public Library, Dún Laoghaire*

_Public Library, Dún Laoghaire, Ireland:_ Spend any length of time in Ireland and you fall for its charms. Our competition entry for the Dún Laoghaire Library was in part homage to what I perceived to be the spirit of the Irish: a warm, generous people with a staggering gift of the gab and a universally shared deep pride in and connection to their literature. A library for these people in the heartland of Joyce and Beckett seemed a beautiful proposition.

The building was to be located on the edge of an existing park flanked by two church spires, with a commanding aspect over the famous harbour that is locked in the grip of two kilometre-long piers that stretch out into Dublin Bay. The park contained an oval pond, a relic of the steamship days when it provided the fresh water for the ferries taking the many thousand emigrants to Britain. The whole site is a street away from the local high street and a coast road away from the Carlisle Pier. It is overlooked by the grand Royal Marine Hotel.

I found myself wanting to keep the openness of the site, wanting to keep the dialogue between the church spires and the dominance of the hotel, but to make much more of the park and its connection to the piers and promenade into the sea. All projects tend to be an amalgam of previous ideas locked into a new form.

I exploited the five metre difference in height from Haight Terrace down to the park to insert the library at park level but below the datum of the terrace. We then proposed a new wildlife sanctuary at terrace level that covered the roof of the library. The roof therefore became a small wildlife reserve with indigenous plants that would attract coastal birdlife and that could be visited along boardwalks.

The main library was laid out around the oval of the previous pond, in the same way as the Piazza Navona was laid out around the Roman Stadium of Domitian. At the centre of the inner court, accessed across four radiating bridges, was the place where readers could interact with library staff, the soul of the library. The reading and study rooms radiated out from that hub. The edge of the upper level was ringed with an oval circulation for perambulation and interaction. I borrowed lessons learnt from St Marylebone's concrete construction and integrated it with sustainable servicing methods to create an extremely low-energy and naturally lit Library.

But the key move was outside the facility. We carved a sinuous new pedestrian street into this invented landscape, a small ravine heading for the sea, its delta forming a natural spot for groups to meet and hang out before heading for the library or the high street or for a

_Opposite_
The Public Library is conceived within a new overall public realm that links the high street to the Carlisle Pier, leaving the openness of the site intact and the park restored and renewed.

*Public Library, Dún Laoghaire*

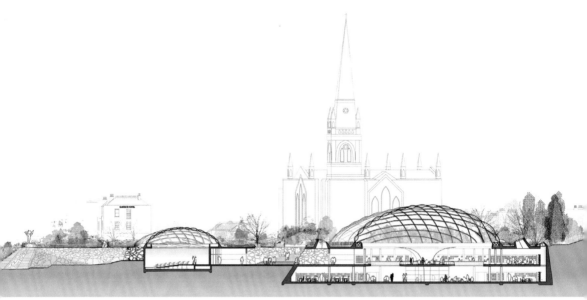

promenade along the pier. The oval court was covered by a semi-transparent golden polytetrafluoroethylene (PTFE) roof on a lightweight timber latticework that symbolised the pride of the community and broadcast the presence of the cultural treasures beneath.

*Opposite top*
The library takes advantage of the large change in level and re-creates a parkland on its roof that is now at street level. The building is naturally cooled by the ground and receives controlled daylight from rooflights.

*Opposite middle*
At the heart of the Library is the information hub where knowledge is exchanged. Each reading room connects to an open ambulatory that allows for serendipitous meetings.

*Opposite bottom*
The golden PTFE roof of the library heralds the importance of the cultural building from Dublin Bay.

*Tread Lightly, Lesser Caucasus:* Being of Armenian descent but never having ventured to Armenia, despite a life-long respect for its historic architecture, I was eager to attend the explorer Tom Allen's lecture at the Royal Geographic Society. In a packed theatre of wildly enthusiastic listeners, Tom and his colleagues described their journeys across the mountains and their aim to secure an international-quality hiking route that, politics permitting, would eventually connect Iran to Georgia and Turkey to Azerbaijan.

As I listened, I grew excited by the idea of expanding the trail into a type of cultural route not dissimilar to the Camino de Santiago in Spain, the Kumano Kodo in Japan and the Ruta del Peregrino in Mexico. The urgency of the idea was reinforced by the pattern of population drift, amongst the young in particular, from mountain villages to the cities, and the then government's commitment to expanding conventional tourism serviced from the growing capital, Yerevan.

I already knew the quality of Armenia's ancient architecture, but I was taken aback by the variety and beauty of its landscapes and the tales of hospitality of the local people. I spoke to Tom about expanding the ambition of the project and we resolved to meet on the foothills of the Armenian Alps, Dilijan National Park in the Lesser Caucasus. Over a period of four days Tom and I scouted 25km of territory to locate sites for pilot architectural interventions.

It was immediately clear that the jewel-like churches and monuments would soon be overwhelmed by coachloads of tourists who would come and go without spending their dollars in the local community. The suggestion was to spread the new tourist load across the wilderness and amongst the mountain people. The trail was, by definition, off the beaten track and it would consequently be easier for local communities to retain any money they might thus earn. My argument was that, with careful planning and strategic cultural interventions, the trail could be of an exceptional international standard and become an umbrella for the many diverse but complementary initiatives that are continuously instigated from the diaspora. To my mind it would ultimately create a greater impact than the sum of its parts and not least empower the local communities. Such an approach could lead to many positive offshoots: derelict village homes converted and managed by locals for bed-and-breakfast accommodation; pop-up restaurants run by young chefs in villages along the route using artisanal produce grown specially by local farmers; a renaissance in wine-growing in what

*Opposite*
Scouting the Dilijan National Park with Tom Allen for potential sites for strategic interventions.

*Tread Lightly, Lesser Caucasus*

experts describe as perfect terroir; a venue for music, food and theatre festivals and, most importantly, the protection and husbandry of the land.

Tom and I developed our 'Tread Lightly' pilot projects with this ambition in mind. We selected five sites that we felt celebrated the essence of each place, and which could support activities that drew people together and closer to this magnificent landscape and culture. We imagined the trail being regularly used by school parties and groups of walkers, so located temporary structures in the ruins of hamlets along the route to provide refuge. We invited the Yerevan architecture schools to hold annual design competitions for temporary shelters to be erected by students and volunteers.

Dilijan is rich in mineral waters and we envisaged a regular sequence of drinking fountains sponsored by local water companies that would create rest points where people could meet, and that would obviate the need for disposable plastic bottles that litter so many tourist landscapes.

We imagined a waterfall shaped into onsen-style pools for bathing and relaxing. The programme also has serious didactic, environmental objectives. A famous local lake, a popular picnic destination, had had its reed beds and banks levelled to create flat ground for picnickers to better access the spot by car. When we visited only a few months after its desecration, the previously crystal-clear waters had already begun to turn green and its wildlife support system degrade. Our proposals set out how to integrate wildlife and people, restore the banks of the lake and introduce boardwalks and pontoons to allow access and enjoyment of the tranquillity and beauty of the spot without causing its destruction.

We envisaged a covered open-air amphitheatre 3km from the nearest village as the venue for an annual moonlit festival featuring musicians from the local community and the national conservatoire. The audience would walk to the theatre in daylight and return under the stars. The amphitheatre was formed in a natural dip in the side of a hill that was surmounted by the ruins of an ancient church.

The most spectacular of all the proposals was a serpentine ropebridge designed by the brilliant Matthew Wells of Techniker who engineered a structure of lightweight components small enough to be carried to the site and assembled by hand. Once assembled the bridge, strung from opposing banks, suspended the walker in mid-air over an otherwise impassable gorge.

*Opposite*
The spectacular serpentine bridge snakes its way across gorge suspending the walker in mid-air. Experiences such as this open up the landscape to the visitor and could make the Transcaucasian Trail an unmissable part of any visit to Armenia.

Thanks to the generous patronage of Yvonne Farrell and Shelley MacNamara, the brilliant architects and directors of the 2018 Architectural Biennale, 'Tread Lightly' was exhibited in the beautiful 12th-century Corderie in the Venice Arsenale. We used the opportunity to express the project manifesto by making our first site-specific installation: what we called a small chapel for five proposals set on plinths of rammed Venetian clays that harmonised with the great columns of the building. These were to be given to Venice as permanent planters for pomegranate trees, the symbol of Armenia.

'Tread Lightly' joins up many of the social and environmental themes of this book and helps to outline a way that many of us practise architecture: always aiming beyond the strict requirements of the brief to deliver greater all-round effect and character.

When an architectural project achieves this greater public good, I call it 'civil' architecture, a term entirely borrowed from the RIBA's 1837 Charter. Its founders defined the purpose of the new institute as the advancement of civil architecture, as an art esteemed in all enlightened nations to promote the domestic convenience of citizens and the public improvement and embellishment of towns and cities.

At a time in our history when style so often outshines substance, the then director of the Award Programme, Tony Chapman and I chose this term as the new criterion for the RIBA International Prize that we launched in 2016, some 180 years after the RIBA's foundation. This prescient Victorian worldview takes in social respect and environmental responsibility. As the nations of the world together face the challenge of creating ever-greater cities on ever more depleted territories, these ambitions remain poignantly relevant.

For me, architecture should aim beyond the delivery of function or beauty. We need architecture to provide our shelter, to embrace our communities and to celebrate our landscapes, but we also need architecture to continuously challenge us by mapping out better futures.

For me this is the fundamental point of architecture.

*Opposite*
The first site-specific intervention of the 'Tread Lightly' project in the 12th-century Corderie in Venice. The plinths were made of local gravels and clays that echo the colours and textures of the Corderie's magnificent Doric brick columns. Five exhibits illustrate the pilot projects for the Dilijan National Park, Armenia.

My favourite client begins every design review with an exposé of the issues and leaves every meeting with the simple instruction: 'Do your best'. I love the acuity and implicit trust. This is the model for client/architect collaboration and is deeply empowering.

Problem-solving is hard-wired into the architect's approach to the world, and it comforts us to think that our buildings are the silver bullets that can face off the crisis of modern alienation and environmental degradation. But in truth the crisis that faces society is an amalgam of multitudinous activities that can only be addressed by restoring some form of unified common sense and some renewed consideration for others, by 'making every decision personal', as my wife Eliza tirelessly expounds.

Though not the solution, architecture is nonetheless extremely well placed to contribute to the process of reversing our destructive trends, not least by signalling incremental ways forward. In this respect, design awards remain a key and powerful tool for giving oxygen to new ideas and for urgently disseminating those ideas within the profession and to the general public.

Architecture touches areas far broader than its perceived realm of influence. This is because the everyday practice of architecture involves us in collaboration with multitudes of fellow professionals, manufacturers, contractors, civil servants and politicians. It importantly brings us into direct contact with real people, real families, real organisations and, most critically, the ground itself.

The reach and focus of architecture can be as wide-ranging as we want it to be — hence it remains for me the most open, useful and fascinating of disciplines.

Sensing Place, or meticulously judging and intuiting the best future for a particular place or community, is at the heart of my approach to architecture. My small body of work has the big ambition of celebrating place and of nurturing people to tread lightly on the land that Buckminster Fuller so perceptively called 'our Spaceship Earth'.

Born in 1958, Philip Gumuchdjian graduated from the University of East Anglia, the Architectural Association and the Royal College of Art. He began his career in the Richard Rogers studio in 1980 where he worked for 18 years. He co-wrote Richard Rogers's book on sustainable urban development, *Cities for a small planet*, published by Faber & Faber, and in 1986 designed the influential 'London as it could be' exhibition at the Royal Academy.

In 1998 he set up his own firm, Gumuchdjian Architects, and designed the Think Tank in Ireland, the Giant Recycled Paper Building in the Millennium Dome, the Marylebone Performing Arts Centre in London and the controversial Tower by the Tate Modern. In 2003, with Shigeru Ban and Jean de Gastines, he won the international competition for the satellite Centre Georges Pompidou in Metz which was completed in 2010. Current projects include new residential buildings in London's Glebe Place, Pembridge Crescent, Old Church Street and Richmond Hill, as well as in Sotogrande, Spain, and a new cultural trail in the Lesser Caucasus. He recently completed the restoration of Rogers's 1968 Parkside building for the Harvard Graduate School of Design.

The firm has received a number of architecture and industry accolades, including the Stephen Lawrence Award in 2003 and 2010 and the RIBA International award in 2012. Philip was selected to exhibit his 'Tread Lightly' project at the 2018 Venice Architecture Biennale and was keynote speaker at the Buenos Aires Architecture Biennale 2018.

*Gumuchdjian Architects selected works* was published by Eight Books in 2009. In 2019 and accompanying the publication of this book, a one-man show at Messums Wiltshire exhibited 'Sensing Place', 20 years of the practice's output.

Philip was Rapporteur at the UN Habitat II conference in Istanbul, a member of the Urban 21 panel and has taught Urban Design at the Bartlett School of Architecture. He chaired the RIBA Awards Group from 2016 to 2018, and was a member of the jury for the relaunched RIBA International Prize.

Collaborators

**ARCHITECTS**
John Andrews
Shigeru Ban
Kevin Dash
Formation Architects
Jean de Gastines
Annabelle Selldorf
Stephen Spence
Svarquitecte
Touza Arquitectos

**LANDSCAPE**
Jonnie Bell
Michel Desvignes
Todd Longstaffe-Gowan
Jean Mus
Tom Stuart-Smith

**INTERIORS**
Owen Design
Jean-Louis Deniot
MHZ

**STRUCTURE**
Arup
AKT2
Buro Happold
Allan Conisbee
Expedition Engineering
Anthony Hunt
Techniker

**SERVICES**
Arup
Atelier Ten
Fulcrum Services
Hoare Lea
IDA
Richard Pearce
ZEF

**ARTISTS**
Anish Kapoor
Langlands & Bell
Dante Leonelli
Noble & Webster
Eduardo Paolozzi
William Peers
Sarah Raphael
Cosima Spender
Georgina Starr
Mark Wallinger
Richard Wilding
Richard Wilson

**HERITAGE**
Alan Baxter
Sherban Cantcuzino
John Harris
Chris Miele
Paddy Pugh
Tavernor
Paul Velluet

**PLANNING**
DP9
Lichfields
Savills

**QUANTITY SURVEYORS**
Aecom
Kevin Bonfield
Fanshawe
Paul Ginger
Gleeds
Robert Maxwell
Sawyer & Fisher
Woodeson Drury

**ASSOCIATES**
Shinya Mouri
Ralf Eikelberg
Robert Bourke
Daniel Glaessl
Matthias Piper
Lucinda Parrish
Byron Bassington

**TEAM**
Carmen Acosta
Nigel Allen
Camilo Alvarado
Takashi Arimoto
Christopher Arnold
Emma Bailey
Lara Baitarian
Ryan Beecroft
Andres Besomi
Elisa Bodigoi
Jayne Breakwell
Robert Browne
Edoardo Capecci
Giulia Carboni
Atisthan Charoenkool
Shant Charoian
George Chidiac
Shaun Siu Chong
Borja Colom
Caitlin Comrie
Anne Marie Diderich
Yvonne Ebmier
Subomi Fapohunda
Roberto Fardelli
Catarina Felicio
Eva Friedrich
Clara Gade
Adrian Garcia Buey
Giorgio Gilbini
Chiara Hall

Amy Hallett
Anna Hastings
Meriel Hunt
Vytautas Jackus
Darren Kaye
Wayne Kelsall
Katsura Leslie
Sybil Lienert
Goncalo Lopes
Chiara Luzzato
Martina Meluzzi
Catalina Mendez
Vahagn Mkrtchyan
Jake Moulson
Siebrine Noordenbos
Stefano Piedimonte
Andrew Pledge
Michael Ramwell
Miguel Reyna
Rafael Sanchez
Dinani Saraswati
Claudia Schmidt
Tony Schonhardt
Julian Siravo
Paul Skinner
Bobby Small
Charlotte Smith
Emil Torday
Ruth Torday
Maria Torres
Stefano Vafiadis
Varudh Varavarn
Peter Webb
Anna Zaniboni

Laurie Abbott  Nick Adler  Isabel Allen  Tom Allen  Martine d'Anglejan-Chatillon
Martin & Rose Armstrong  Gokhan Avcioglu  Amanda Bailleu  David Baldwin  Shigeru Ban
Katy Barker  Rachel Barraclough  Alessandra Finotto & Luca Bechis
Ahmed & Abeer Ben Halim  Dorothy Berwin  Hannah Betts  Richie Bieniasz  Marcus Binney
Michael Bithell  Anthony Blee  Laurent le Bon  Valerio Bonelli  Bruce Bossom  Dominic Bradbury
Jeremy & Karen Brade  Greg Bradford  Wes Bradford  Stefano Bucci  Jonathan Buchanan
Katherine Butler  Sir Michael Butler  Pamela Buxton  Sue Carpenter  Stella Cattana
Will Champion  Tony Chapman  Evgeny Chmutov  Clemency Christopherson  Olivier Cinqualbre
Richard Collins  Adrian Cooper  Frederick Cooper  Peter Crane  Brian Cuthbertson
Thomas Dane  Kevin & Angela Dash  Lou Dasserville  Simon Dasserville  Peter Davey
Mike Davies  Richard Davies  Sophie Dawson  Paul de Meo  Richard & Adeela de Unger
Anthony Denselow  Andrew Derrick  Michel Desvignes  Claudia Downs  Thomas Drexel
Anthony Dunnett  Veronique Economou  Helen Edwards  Lynsday Edwards  Barrie Evans
Ben Evans  Homa Farjadi  Yvonne Farrell  Mark Fletcher  Regis & Valentine Franc
Robert Friedland  Bill Garvey  Dominique Gauzin-Mueller  Matthew Gibbs
Dieter & Beatrix Gilomen  Herbert Girardet  Jonathan Glancey  Marco Goldschmied
Alberto Gorbatt  Kim Gottlieb  James Gowan  Bennie Gray  Neil Gregory  Lucie Gumuchdjian
Britta Harper  Peter Harris  Sara Hart  Joji Hatori  John & Lorraine Head  Richard Hierons
Chris Hillier  Robin Hodges  Robert Hradsky  Jennifer Hudson  Angela Huntbach  Jon Hunter
John & Mary Hurley  Val Ismaili  Andrew Jackson  Damian Jaques  Joanna Johnston  Kitty Jones
Tracey Josephs  Natalie Kancheli  Jennifer Kean  Giles Kime  Robin Klassnik  Henry & Mo Korda
Aref Lahham  Elizabeth Lambert  Christine & Pierre Lamond  Emmanuelle & Hugues Lepic
Alex Lifshutz  Dan Macarie  Nicholas MacDonald-Buchanan  Vicki MacGregor  Michael Manser
Carmen Mateu  Ingo Maurer  Nick McDowell  Penny McGuire  David McHugh  Niall McLauglin
Shelley McNamara  Jay Merrick  Johnny Messsum  Mike Metcalfe  Catherine Milner
Azmi & Mira Mikati  Rowan Moore  Jasper Morrison  Mohsen Mostafavi  Peter Murray
Stephen & Suzy Murphy  Jo Murtagh  Willie Nickerson  Matthew Orr  Jenny Page
Robin & Lucinda Parish  James Payne  Hugh Pearman  John Perkins  Elizabeth Phillips
Charlotte Philipps  John Pickford  Hans Pietsch  Nicholas People
Eliza Poklewski-Koziell  Ken Powell  Elfreda Pownall  David & Patsy Puttnam  Julienne Ramsauer
Anthony Reynolds  Phyllis Richardson  Patricia Roberts  Siebyl Robson  Richard & Ruthie Rogers
Matias & Mimo Rojas  Norman Rosenthal  Nick Ross  Victoria Lady de Rothschild
Jon Rowlandson  Ray Ryan  William Salomon  Claire Sampson  Jeremy Sandelson
Daman Sanders  John Scott  Stephen Shaffer  Mark Shuttleworth  Colin Singleton
John & Frances Sorrell  Mike Staples  Suzanne Stephens  Peter Stewart  Sachiko Tamashige
Susanne Tamborini  David Tanguy  David Taylor  Byron Thorne  Marc Topiol  Robert Torday
Antonello Vagge  Eric & Lynn Van Peterson  Vlad Vertisiuk  Simon & Amadea West
Jane Withers  Martin White  Nicholas & Cristina White  Robert White  Steve White
Iwan & Manuela Wirth  Dan Witchel  Harry Wolton  Ellis Woodman  Bill Woolf  Inigo Woolf
Jan Woroniecki  John Young  Nir Zamek  Jonathan Zimmerman

GUMUCHDJIAN ARCHITECTS
17 Rosebery Avenue
London EC1R 4SP

Tel +44 (0) 20 7837 1800
www.gumuchdjian.com

PHOTOGRAPHY CREDITS

| | |
|---|---|
| Ben Allen | 180 |
| Iwan Baan | 64–65 |
| Ben Blossom | 99, 146 |
| Richard Bryant | 132–133 |
| David Cleveland | 93 |
| Richard Davies | 16, 19, 36–37, 52, 83, 86, 91, 134, 138, 140, 142, 152–153, 156, 176 |
| Mirjam Devriendt | 56 |
| Chizuko Fletcher | 110 |
| Hufton + Crow | 170, 172–173 |
| Werner Hutmacher | 18, 20, 22, 97 |
| Christoph Kicherer | 174 |
| Peter Krejci Photography | 60 |
| James Merrell | 106, 108, 114 |
| Sandro Michahelles | 80 |
| Ste Murray | 184 |
| Alistair Nicholls | 88, 89, 90, 101, 112–113 |
| Kate Owen | 150, 186 |
| Heiko Prigge | 24 |
| Morley von Sternberg | 82, 148–149 |
| Luke White | 84, 85, 87, 98 |

IMAGE CREDITS

| | |
|---|---|
| Hayes Davidson | 26–27, 162–163 |
| Joseph Robson, AVR | 122 |
| David Rossman | 70 |
| Visualisation One | 38, 42 |
| Vyonyx | 40–41 |
| Steve Whitten | 158, 178 |